TIN CAN SAILORS
WWII

W9-ASW-216

THE FRUGAL SUPERPOWER

ALSO BY MICHAEL MANDELBAUM

*The Nuclear Question: The United States
and Nuclear Weapons, 1946–1976* (1979)

*The Nuclear Revolution: International
Politics Before and After Hiroshima* (1981)

The Nuclear Future (1983)

Reagan and Gorbachev (coauthor, 1987)

*The Fate of Nations: The Search for
National Security in the Nineteenth
and Twentieth Centuries* (1988)

The Global Rivals (coauthor, 1988)

The Dawn of Peace in Europe (1996)

*The Ideas That Conquered the World: Peace, Democracy,
and Free Markets in the Twenty-first Century* (2002)

*The Meaning of Sports: Why Americans Watch Baseball,
Football, and Basketball and What They See
When They Do* (2004)

*The Case for Goliath: How America Acts as the World's
Government in the Twenty-first Century* (2006)

*Democracy's Good Name: The Rise and Risks of the World's
Most Popular Form of Government* (2007)

THE

FRUGAL SUPERPOWER

---

*America's Global Leadership
in a Cash-Strapped Era*

MICHAEL MANDELBAUM

PUBLICAFFAIRS
New York

Copyright © 2010 by Michael Mandelbaum

Published in the United States by PublicAffairs™, a member of the
Perseus Books Group.

All rights reserved.
Printed in the United States of America.

No part of this book may be reproduced in any manner whatsoever
without written permission except in the case of brief quotations
embodied in critical articles and reviews. For information, address
PublicAffairs, 250 West 57th Street, Suite 1321, New York, NY
10107.

PublicAffairs books are available at special discounts for bulk
purchases in the U.S. by corporations, institutions, and other
organizations. For more information, please contact the Special
Markets Department at the Perseus Books Group, 2300 Chestnut
Street, Suite 200, Philadelphia, PA 19103, call (800) 810-4145, ext.
5000, or e-mail special.markets@perseusbooks.com.

Text set in Janson

Library of Congress Cataloging-in-Publication Data

Mandelbaum, Michael.
   The frugal superpower : America's global leadership in a cash-
strapped era / Michael Mandelbaum.
     p. cm.
   Includes index.
   ISBN 978-1-58648-916-8 (alk. paper)
   1. United States—Foreign relations—21st century. 2. Budget—
United States. 3. Finance, Public—United States. I. Title.
   JZ1480.M3259 2010
   327.73—dc22
                                          2010014453
First Edition
10 9 8 7 6 5 4 3 2 1

To my esteemed colleague,
Fouad Ajami,
and to his friend and my beloved wife,
Anne Mandelbaum.

CONTENTS

Contents

ACKNOWLEDGMENTS

The Frugal Superpower began as an address on the future of American foreign policy to the New York Alumni Club of the Johns Hopkins University School of Advanced International Studies (SAIS) on November 13, 2008. I am grateful to the SAIS Development Office and to the School's New York alumni for making it possible and to Lee Kempler for playing host to the event. I developed some of the themes of this book in a talk to the staff of Baraboo Growth LLC in Milwaukee on March 31, 2009. I am indebted to the firm's president, Richard Strong, for the invitation and for his hospitality.

This is my fifth book with PublicAffairs. As with the previous four, I owe a great deal to its founder and editor-at-large, Peter Osnos, not least for having, as he did with the other four, thought of the title for this one. I am grateful to the president of PublicAffairs, Susan Weinberg, and especially to Clive Priddle, whose editorial suggestions substantially improved the manuscript. Melissa Raymond, Meredith Smith, and Antoinette Smith supervised the book's production and Jaime Leifer expertly managed the publicity for it.

Once again I am happy to express my thanks to my peerless agent, Morton L. Janklow, for his wise counsel. I benefitted from conversations on the subjects addressed in these pages with Thomas L. Friedman of *The New York Times* and James Klurfeld of the State University of New York at Stony Brook. My greatest debt, as always, is to my wife, Anne Mandelbaum, for her intellectual stimulation, her matchless editorial judgment, her enthusiastic encouragement, her unwavering support, and her love.

INTRODUCTION

On December 1, 2009, Barack Obama, the forty-fourth American president, delivered a speech at the U.S. Military Academy at West Point, New York. The purpose of the speech was to announce the dispatch of 30,000 additional troops to Afghanistan, where American armed forces had been fighting since 2001. In this sense, the address was an exercise in continuity: all of Obama's predecessors over seven decades, beginning with the thirty-fifth president, Franklin D. Roosevelt, had had occasion to send American military personnel to distant lands.

Yet Obama's remarks, properly understood, marked a sharp and momentous break with the pattern Roosevelt established and all of his successors followed. For even as he ordered the troops to Afghanistan

Obama sought to place limits on the duration of their stay and the mission they would be carrying out, and he made it clear that the reason for these limits was that America could not afford to do more. The most important theme of his remarks was the acknowledgment of economic constraints on American foreign policy, a theme very seldom heard from an American president since Roosevelt took the United States into World War II.

Obama rejected "goals that are beyond what can be achieved at a reasonable cost." He invoked "the connection between our national security and our economy." He cited the need to "rebuild our strength here at home." The only president he quoted was Dwight Eisenhower—of all the chief executives since Franklin Roosevelt the one most committed to limiting the costs of American foreign policy—and the words of Eisenhower's that he cited, which referred to national security policy, were these: "Each proposal must be weighed in the light of a broader consideration: the need to maintain balance in and among national programs."

As if to emphasize Obama's message of economic constraints on foreign policy, the congressional opponents of adding to American troop strength in Afghanistan proposed a special war tax to pay for it. The war was being funded by borrowed money, and its opponents understood that if the American public had to pay for it directly and immediately, out of their own pockets, they might well refuse to do so.

While the economic limits to which Obama referred will directly affect the foreign policy of the United States, their ultimate impact on the rest of the world is likely to be, if anything, even greater. As the president noted at West Point, "More than any other nation, the United States of America has underwritten global security for six decades." Other countries have come to depend on a robust, ambitious, and extensive American foreign policy. The impending economic constraints will place in jeopardy the global tasks that the United States has performed since the 1940s; and what the United States has done has contributed greatly to global peace and prosperity.

When Barack Obama was elected in 2008 he and his supporters expected that his presidency would transform the United States. In one way, at least— but not in a way that so many hoped—that will be the case. Mounting domestic economic obligations will narrow the scope of American foreign policy in the second decade of the twenty-first century and beyond. Because the United States will have to spend so much more than it has in the past on obligations at home—particularly caring for the ever increasing ranks of its older citizens—it will be able to spend less than in the past on foreign policy. Because it will be able to spend less, it will be able to do less. Just what the United States will and will not do will be the most important issue in international relations in the years ahead. It is the subject of *The Frugal Superpower*.

The book's first chapter describes the growing claims on the American budget. They stem not only from the cost of coping with the financial meltdown of 2008 and the subsequent recession but also, and above all, from the expenses of the country's entitlement programs, Social Security and Medicare, which will rise rapidly to historic highs with the retirement of the baby boom generation of Americans born between 1946 and 1964.

Two aspects of the pressure to cut back on foreign policy expenditures that these rapidly mounting domestic costs will exert are particularly notable, and Chapter Two spells them out. First, while they may be normal for most countries most of the time, serious economic constraints on foreign policy did not affect the United States for almost seven decades before 2008. Second, such constraints will affect not only the United States but the entire world because the United States has played an historically unprecedented global role, functioning as the world's de facto government. In an era of scarcity for American foreign policy, the world will get less governance.

Scarcity may, to be sure, bring with it some benefits. It will make the foreign policy of the United States less prone to serious errors. As discussed in Chapter Three, the enormous post–Cold War American margin of superiority in usable power over all other countries bred a certain carelessness that led to two major errors: the ill-advised eastward expansion of the Western military alliance in Europe, the North Atlantic Treaty Organization (NATO), and the disastrously incompetent occupation of Iraq. Less constructively, economic constraints will cause the United States to abandon some of the international services it furnished in the first two post–Cold War decades. It will no longer provide as large a market for other countries' exports. It will almost certainly launch no further military interventions that require costly, protracted, and frustrated exercises in state-building, like the operations in Afghanistan and Iraq.

Abandoning these policies will still leave the United States with formidable international commitments, of which the most important will be ensuring security in Europe and East Asia, opposing the spread of nuclear weapons, and guaranteeing a secure geopolitical background for international commerce, including continuing global access to oil. Chapter Three also explains why it is that, while other countries benefit enormously from these policies, they will not give America much help in carrying them out.

The most serious consequence of a reduced American international role would be a major war. The two countries capable of provoking one are Russia and China. With the exception of the United States, their foreign policies will do more to shape international relations in the second decade of the twenty-first century and beyond than any other country. The uncertain prospects for Chinese and Russian foreign policy are the subject of the book's fourth chapter.

Each of these countries derives more benefit from existing international political and especially economic arrangements than either is likely to achieve by attempting forcibly to alter them. Yet at the same time both have some capacity to disturb the international peace, and each has motives for doing so. Neither is entirely satisfied with the distribution of wealth, power, authority, or even territory globally and particularly in its home region. Whether, how, and to what extent Russia or China or both seek to take advantage of the new limits on American foreign policy is the most important question hanging over international relations in the second decade of the twenty-first century.

Even if China and Russia practice the self-restraint each has generally displayed in the first two decades of the post–Cold War period, one region will continue to require the active, costly engagement of the United States. That region is the Middle East, the subject of Chapter Five. It is both politically unstable and, because it harbors most of the world's easily accessible oil, economically vital. Past American efforts to transform the region to make it more peaceful and so decrease the cost of American operations there have failed.

However, a different way to lower the costs of carrying out its responsibilities in the Middle East is available to the United States: a substantial reduction in the American consumption of oil through a major increase, via taxation, in the price Americans pay for gasoline. No single measure, in fact, would do as much to secure American interests worldwide in the face of the new economic limits on American foreign policy than a large reduction in American oil consumption. Mustering the political will to achieve this goal looms as the single most important foreign policy test the United States will face in the coming age of scarcity.

However the nation performs on that test, American foreign policy will change in a fundamental way. For almost seven decades following the outbreak of World War II, in deciding what policies to pursue beyond their own borders Americans almost never asked themselves the first question that every other country had to address: how much will this cost?

The United States was the billionaire among the world's countries and, unlike the others, operated free of the need to distinguish carefully between necessities and luxuries. If building another missile or aircraft carrier or rescuing a particular country was deemed important, the United States could afford to do it. The international activities of ordinary countries are restrained by, among other things, the need to devote the bulk of their collective resources to domestic projects, such as roads, schools, pensions, and health care. For decades, the United States was exceptional in remaining largely free of such restraints, and the foreign policies that this freedom made possible did a great deal to shape the world of the twenty-first century.

That era is now ending. In the future the United States will behave more like an ordinary country. The pages that follow explore the consequences, for both the United States itself and the rest of the world, of the end of this kind of American exceptionalism.

CHAPTER ONE

—

THE TYRANNY OF NUMBERS

A NEW ERA

September 15, 2008, is an important date in the economic history of the United States, and indeed the entire world. On that day the New York–based international investment bank Lehman Brothers collapsed, creating a panic in the nation's financial system and an immense loss of wealth, and deepening an already serious global economic downturn. That day is also significant, however, for the history of American foreign policy.

What happened on September 15, 2008, accelerated a series of developments that will change the resources at the disposal of policy-makers in Washington, limiting the financial means available to conduct American foreign policy. The events of that day, in combination with trends in the American economy that were already under way and will expand in the years ahead, will reduce what the United States does in the world.

Because a credit crisis of the kind that the Lehman collapse produced, if severe and prolonged enough, can inflict catastrophic economic damage, the American government took radical steps to counteract it, expanding its role in the financial system to the point that it became, in effect, one of the country's largest banks. The Federal Reserve Board offered loans to institutions that had never before been given them, and the government took control of the American International Group, a multinational insurance company, and two quasi-governmental purchasers of mortgages, known as Fannie Mae and Freddie Mac. The Congress appropriated $750 billion for the purpose of buying up bad housing loans, but the Treasury Department used the money instead to purchase shares in the nation's largest commercial banks, in an effort to keep them solvent and unclog the flow of credit they provide. Despite these extraordinary efforts, with banks fearful of lending and consumers

fearful of buying, the American economy, and economies all around the world, fell into a deep recession,
the worst since the greatest and most destructive economic downturn of modern history, the Great Depression of the 1930s.

In addition to the impact on the American and
global economies, all this will eventually affect the
foreign policy of the United States. For one thing, it
shook Americans' confidence in their government's
capacity for economic management, and confidence
in government is crucial for foreign policy, which is,
after all, conducted almost exclusively by the government. For another, in times of economic crisis Americans, like people everywhere, tend to turn inward
and devote more attention and resources to their own
concerns than to problems beyond their borders.
Still, the country experienced recessions after the Depression, including during the Cold War, which did
not materially affect America's major international
commitments.

What makes September 15, 2008, important for
the history of American foreign policy is not simply
the financial crisis that the Lehman collapse crystal-
lized, or the recession that it dramatically worsened,
but rather the impact of these developments in combination with the principal economic challenges that

the United States will have to confront in the twenty-first century, in particular the benefits promised to older Americans, the ranks of which will swell in the years ahead. Together they will vastly expand the economic obligations of the American federal government, which will in turn narrow the scope of foreign policy by diminishing the resources available for it.

In the immediate aftermath of the economic crisis of 2008, as well as in the years thereafter, one economic challenge destined to weigh heavily on American foreign policy is the nation's debt, a challenge severely aggravated by the deep recession set off by the September 15 collapse. During recessions the revenues flowing to the government in the form of taxes decrease; people lose their jobs and therefore their incomes and so don't pay taxes. At the same time, federal expenditures increase as programs that recessions trigger, such as unemployment insurance, grow larger.

The standard remedy for fighting recessions is deficit spending—expenditures funded not by tax revenues but by federal borrowing—and the American government applied that remedy liberally. In early 2009 the Congress approved a $780 billion package of programs designed to stimulate economic activity in the United States. All of the money to be spent was borrowed rather than raised through taxing the

American people. The deficit for fiscal year 2009 reached $1.4 trillion, fully 10 percent of an economy with a total annual value of about $14 trillion, and much higher than the 3 percent widely considered the maximum "safe" annual deficit. Moreover, the country faced the prospect of comparably large gaps between expenditures and revenues in the years ahead. The fiscal year 2010 deficit was projected to be $1.6 trillion. By the estimate of the Congressional Budget Office, annual deficits might well average more than $1 trillion every year for a full decade after 2009.

These deficits will be added to a cumulative national debt—the total of annual deficits—of about $9 trillion, much of it compiled between 2001 (when it stood at $5.6 trillion) and 2007 through generous tax cuts, expanded federal programs, and a war in Iraq, the ultimate cost of which will certainly approach $2 trillion and may be closer to $3 trillion. A phrase often attributed to the Republican leader in the U.S. Senate in the 1960s, Everett M. Dirksen, in describing what he considered his colleagues' profligate spending habits is appropriate in this context: "A billion here, a billion there, and pretty soon you're talking about real money." Even allowing for inflation, the government's tendency to spend has grown dramatically since Dirksen's time: a trillion is a thousand times a billion. In Dirksen's day, however, the government was in the habit of paying for its expenditures with tax revenues. Since then it has done so through borrowing: in the forty-seven years before 2008, the federal budget was balanced—that is, government income matched or exceeded outlays—in only five of them.

Although payment is deferred, borrowing comes at a price. The interest charge on the national debt must be paid every year: the greater the debt, the higher will be the cost of servicing it. That cost will reach 10 percent of the total federal budget by 2011 and 17 percent of total revenues by 2019, by relatively conservative estimates. If interest rates rise sharply it could be more. What the country spends on interest on the national debt it cannot spend on anything else, including foreign policy. Moreover, if lenders lose confidence in the federal government's ability to pay back what it borrows, the cost of its loans—the interest rate on government securities—will rise, further increasing the national debt. By the third decade of the twenty-first century the cost to American taxpayers of servicing the national debt is scheduled to exceed the entire defense budget.

Debt in and of itself is not a bad thing. To the contrary, households, firms, and countries routinely borrow money. Debt is the fuel on which any modern economy runs. But the pattern of borrowing in which the United States has engaged for almost half a century has three particular features that distinguish what America owes from normal, desirable, economically healthy debt, and those three differences make the American national debt a prospective drain on American foreign policy.

First, prudent debtors use what they borrow for investment, which enhances their incomes, from which they can then both pay off their debts and improve their net worth. Much of what the United States has borrowed over the years, however, has gone to consumption of one kind or another, not to investment.

Second, because the savings of citizens in the United States have been low, the government was forced to borrow a great deal from abroad. Indeed, American debt to other countries helped to sustain global consumption even as other countries, particularly China, saved a great deal. This arrangement underpinned an impressive rate of overall global economic growth for much of the first decade of the twenty-first century. China produced goods and sold them to the United States, which, in effect, paid for them by borrowing back from the Chinese what Americans had paid for those goods.

The arrangement suited all parties involved in the short term, but the dollars that flooded back into the United States from abroad helped to inflate the housing bubble whose bursting triggered the severe economic crisis of 2008. More damaging for American foreign policy is the fact that the arrangement cannot be sustained over the long term: China and other countries will not lend to the United States indefinitely and without limit. Americans will have to consume less and save more, and a dollar saved is a dollar not spent supporting the various foreign policies of the United States.

A third feature of the debt accumulated by the United States has the potential to affect American foreign policy. A highly indebted country is inevitably tempted to print the money it needs to pay its debts. In 2008 the Federal Reserve in fact created several trillion dollars to fund the measures it deemed necessary to prevent a financial collapse. The monetary authorities hope and expect to recoup these outlays by selling, at a propitious time, the assets, such as shares of large banks, that they created the money to acquire. That would withdraw money from the economy. Even in that case, however, the obligation to repay the money the government has borrowed will still remain. Using the printing presses to repay debt, an all too common pattern historically, leads to a devastating economic pathology: inflation. Severe inflation can produce a weak economy, a distracted and demoralized public, and a discredited government, all of which cripple the afflicted country's capacity to act effectively in foreign affairs. The anticipation of inflation, moreover, causes purchasers of government bonds to demand higher interest rates, which further expands the national debt.

Inflation, debt, recession: these are the equivalents for a national economy of illnesses besetting an individual. And just as an individual afflicted with gout, or pneumonia, or heart disease will be less energetic than a fully healthy person, so a country suffering from economic ailments will be less vigorous in its collective pursuits, foreign policy among them. Still, none of these economic maladies is without precedent in American history. The United States encountered and overcame all of them in the past, as recently as during the Cold War, without seriously impairing its foreign policies. Indeed, by some measures the twenty-first-century afflictions are likely to be of historically modest severity. Indebted though the United

States had become by 2008, as a percentage of its total output the country's debt was only half what it had been in 1945, when the cost of waging World War II sent it soaring to 122 percent of the national gross domestic product (GDP). Even with another decade of large annual debts after 2008, the national debt-to-GDP ratio, by at least one calculation, would reach only 80 percent, which would still be lower than that of 1945.

In the two decades after 1945 the government reduced its debt while carrying out a foreign policy of global scope. At the heart of that policy was the political and military contest with the Soviet Union, in which the share of the American GDP devoted to defense routinely reached an annual level twice as high as what it was in the first decade of the twenty-first century. Occasionally it was even three times higher. The effective Cold War combination of a prudent fiscal policy and an expansive foreign policy is unlikely to be repeated in the second and third decades of the present century, however, because of an economic condition of towering, indeed era-defining importance that was largely absent in the post–World War II era. That condition, which, combined with the impact of the economic downturn of 2008 and enormous debt amassed by the American government, will have a decisive impact on the foreign policy of the United States, is the very large bill that will confront the country for expenditures known as entitlements.

ENTITLEMENTS

In America, as in other countries, the government provides pensions and health care for its older citizens. Social Security and Medicare (and Medicaid, for indigent people) had become, by 2008, expensive programs. Added together, their benefits, to which every American age sixty-five or older is entitled (hence "entitlements"), commanded 40 percent of the federal budget. They far outstripped any other single federal expense, including the cost of what has historically been deemed to be every government's first duty, national defense. What is spent on entitlements, like what is spent on debt service, cannot be spent on foreign policy.

Over the preceding half century the American government's priorities, as revealed by the distribution of its expenditures, had undergone a basic shift—from guns to butter. For almost all of history, governments the world over had devoted their resources mainly to building and maintaining the military forces necessary to defend their countries and to pursue whatever military goals they set for themselves beyond their borders. By the first decade of the twenty-first century the federal government of the United States, judging by the pattern of its spending, was well on its way to becoming a giant domestic insurance company, albeit one with a sideline in foreign policy. As expensive as Social Security and Medicare had become by 2008, however, they will be even more expensive in the years ahead. In 2008, all forms of government-supplied pensions and health care (including Medicaid) constituted about 4 percent of total American output; at present rates they will rise steadily for decades until, by 2050, they account for a full 18 percent of everything the United States produces. This growth will fundamentally transform the public life of the United States and therefore the country's foreign policy. The costs of the developments the events of September 15, 2008, triggered, along with the massive increase in the costs of America's entitlement programs, will claim an ever-increasing share of America's national wealth, to the detriment of American foreign policy.

The massive increase will come about because of the eligibility for the benefits of these programs of the so-called baby-boom generation, the largest age cohort in American history. Between 1946 and 1964,

77 million Americans were born. The leading edge of that vast population wave will turn sixty-five, and qualify for most retirement and health care benefits, in 2011; the rest will follow. The government does not have the money needed to pay these benefits. Social Security and Medicare are "unfunded obligations." By the estimate of the Congressional Budget Office, the total cost of these unfunded obligations— the gap between what the government owes and what, at existing levels of taxation, it can expect to collect exceeds $52 trillion—almost four times the output of the entire American economy in 2008. Some estimates are even higher.

The government does not have the money to pay for these programs because, since the inception of Social Security in 1937 and the beginning of Medicare in 1965, they have been funded on a "pay-as-you-go" basis: each generation of workers has paid for the benefits of those who have already retired. As long as the working population comfortably outnumbered retirees, paying for government-supplied pensions and health care was not unduly burdensome for the society as a whole. But the retirement of the baby boomers will turn the age structure of the American population upside down. The ratio of current workers to retirees will fall sharply. The burden on each

worker of supporting the growing population of retirees will, accordingly, rise sharply. To meet these
obligations, assuming that they do not change, taxes
would have to increase by a politically impossible and
economically ruinous 150 percent. To put the trend
in America's fiscal position in historical perspective,
beginning in the second decade of the century the
priorities and obligations of American society will,
over time, change on a scale that, in the past hundred
years, only the Great Depression and World War II
produced. Those two monumental events led to dramatic changes in American foreign policy. So will this
one.

The forecast of a transformation in American economic life and thus in American foreign policy depends in part on a prediction about the size and
composition of the American population in the years
ahead. Demographic predictions tend to be far more
reliable than forecasts concerning other aspects of social life. Birth and death rates change slowly, not
abruptly; and the predictions about the impact of demographics on the costs of entitlement programs are
unusually reliable because the people who will lay
claim to the tens of trillions of dollars in benefits have
already been born. Moreover, their life expectancies,
and thus the benefits they will collect, will only in-

crease. All that is necessary for entitlement costs to soar, therefore, is the simple passage of time.

Entitlement costs will rise for technological as well as demographic reasons. New and better methods of diagnosing and treating diseases are constantly being developed: the United States and other countries spend billions of dollars each year to do exactly that. These new therapies tend to be more expensive than those they replace, driving up the price of health care. Even as more people qualify for government-provided medical benefits, therefore, the price of treatment for each individual will rise. By 2030, by one estimate, public and private spending on health care will reach 41 percent of the income of the average American household. Under these circumstances Americans will seek to reduce spending on other things, including on their support for the nation's foreign policies.

The United States is not the only country that will have to cope with the consequences of an aging society. What is known as the demographic transition—the combination of falling birthrates and longer life expectancies, leading to an older population—is already taking place all over the world. For most rich countries, in fact, the consequences of this transition will be more pronounced than for the United States.

Their birthrates are lower, so not only will their societies age more rapidly, but their total populations
will actually shrink, even as America's continues to
grow because of higher rates of both fertility and im-
migration. The dependency burden—the ratio of retirees to active workers—will rise more rapidly in
other countries than in the United States, imposing
a heavier economic burden on their taxpayers. Many
of these countries already have bigger debts, measured as proportions of total annual output. But the
United States differs from its fellow wealthy countries in two major ways that aggravate the problems
an aging population presents.

First, the impact on foreign policy will be far
greater, because the United States conducts a much
more expansive foreign policy and shoulders considerably greater global responsibilities than do the Europeans or the Japanese. Second, in the first decade
of the twenty-first century income and wealth came
to be more unevenly distributed in the United States
than in other wealthy countries. By one estimate, in
the three decades after 1970 the inflation-adjusted income of the top fifth of American earners rose by 60
percent, while it fell by 10 percent for all others. The
reasons for this inequality, which had increased over
the course of four decades, are complicated and con-

troversial. The most often cited causes are technological change and globalization—the broadening of international trade and capital flows and the shift of jobs from rich countries, such as the United States, to poorer ones where wages are lower. The fact of inequality, combined with the insecurity about jobs and income that globalization has engendered in the United States as in other countries, creates political pressure on the American government to counteract these two trends.

The obvious way to counteract them is to make entitlement programs more rather than less generous. The health care reform measure passed by the Congress and signed by the president in March 2010 testifies to the widely felt impulse for greater public generosity. But the passage of that bill will probably not eliminate public pressure for more extensive (and therefore more expensive) social programs and will certainly not reduce the ever-rising costs of medical care in the United States. The bill will not avoid, and may even increase, further pressure on the nation's non-entitlement expenditures, including foreign policy.

The ways that the aging of the population, in combination with the economic crisis of 2008 and the increase in the country's indebtedness, will affect the public policy of the United States are not foreordained, but two consequences are virtually certain. One is that, in response to the surge in claims on the American government, commitments to retirees will eventually be modified. Americans will have to pay more to fulfill the obligations that the country has assumed. Taxation will ultimately increase, but since fulfilling the nation's obligations, as they stood in 2008, to the letter would raise taxes to a level that would crush the American economy, entitlement programs will also be modified. Twenty-first-century Americans who are sixty-five or older will receive fewer benefits from the government than they have been promised.

Of the two major entitlement programs, Social Security will be the easier to modify—by some combination of raising the retirement age, changing the formula for cost-of-living increases in the stipend, and perhaps taxing the benefits provided to recipients with high incomes. If a group of people knowledgeable about the issue were to convene in a single room, it has been said, it would take them only ten minutes to agree on a formula for restructuring the Social Security program, and it would take that long only because the first seven minutes would be devoted to exchanging pleasantries.

Medicare presents greater economic, political, and indeed moral difficulties: to restrict the growth of its costs will require rationing health care, which will mean denying payment for some therapies to some people, which will cause some of them to die sooner than they would have if the government had paid for all possible treatments. To say that such measures will be controversial is an understatement, and the controversy will unfold where issues of public policy are decided: in the political arena. This leads to the second predictable consequence of the tidal wave of economic obligations that will engulf the United States: it will transform American politics.

Ever since the late nineteenth century, economic policy has played a central and often a defining role in American political life. The Democratic candidate for president in 1896, William Jennings Bryan, who denounced American adherence to the gold standard because it injured western farmers, could easily have adopted the motto of Bill Clinton's campaign slogan almost a hundred years later: "It's the economy, stupid." From 1961 to 1981 the politics of economic policy was dominated by an allegiance to a version of the teachings of John Maynard Keynes, the great English economist of the first half of the twentieth century. According to the then-dominant interpretation of Keynes, downturns in economic output can be prevented, or at least cushioned, by deficit spending by the government. (This strategy was revived by the Obama administration to deal with the economic crisis that began in 2008.) From 1981 to 2008 a different orthodoxy governed economic policy, one that holds that tax cuts are always good for the economy because they always lead to increased production.

Although they differ in significant respects, these two approaches have an important common feature: both lend themselves to ever-higher consumption without ever-higher taxation. Each approach made Americans an offer they could not, and did not, refuse: more spending, both public and private. These circumstances were favorable to those seeking resources to support a wide range of public policies, including foreign policy.

The collapse of 2008, the surge in American indebtedness, and the retirement of the baby boomers with the resulting explosion of claims on the federal government will create a different economic imperative: higher taxes, more saving, and less consumption. This change will reduce the resources available for all public purposes: there will be less to go around. Along with other publicly funded activities, the change will impose new limits on the conduct of foreign policy. It will do so by altering the framework within which American foreign policy is made and carried out.

Foreign Policy Limits

For the American public, matters of foreign policy are more distant and less familiar than domestic issues. Where taxes and government-provided benefits are concerned, Americans tend to have clear views, which they transmit forcefully to their elected representatives. On issues close to home, they feel at home. When it comes to policies toward other countries, the direct stakes for individual citizens seem (and usually are) low. Accordingly, most Americans know little about them and pay only occasional attention to them. Americans organize themselves into sizable, powerful lobbies, to which they contribute time and money on a large scale, to press for direct economic benefits from the government; the lobbies that focus on international affairs are smaller and less powerful.

In foreign policy-making, in fact, the American public is divided into two groups of vastly different sizes: a small one, located mainly on the two coasts and especially concentrated in Washington, D.C., follows international issues closely, writes about and discusses them in the media, and, when its members serve as government officials, sets and carries out the foreign policy of the United States. The much larger majority of the population has far less information, interest, and influence. Foreign policy is the province of the expert. The foreign policy community is the equivalent of a physician, to which the public cedes responsibility for diagnoses and prescriptions governing America's relations with other countries.

This does not mean, however, that on matters of foreign policy the American government can do whatever it wants, or that it is restrained only by the opinions and activities of the members of the foreign policy community who do not hold office. In foreign affairs, as on domestic issues, policies are subject to democratic control. To be sure, the government has wider latitude in initiating foreign policies. But the public ultimately renders a verdict on them, through public opinion polls approving or disapproving of them and, most powerfully, through elections, in which those responsible for the policies are either returned to office or defeated. On matters of foreign policy the public in effect says to the government: You do what you think serves the interests of the United States. After seeing the result, we'll pass judgment on what you've done. If we don't approve, we'll fire you.

The public's verdict is not always favorable. Public officials do get fired. The presidents responsible for initiating the American wars in Korea, Vietnam, and Iraq all suffered public rejection. (In none of these cases did the public oppose the goals on behalf of which the war was being waged—a non-communist South Korea and South Vietnam and a united, stable, democratic, pro-Western Iraq. Instead, Americans concluded that the government was spending too much, in both lives and dollars, in pursuit of those goals.)

Nor is electoral punishment the only constraint on the freedom to manage American foreign policy. The government operates within limits that arise from a broad consensus about what is desirable and what is feasible for the United States. During the Cold War, for example, it scrupulously avoided measures likely to bring the country into direct military conflict with the Soviet Union, for that would have sharply increased the chance of a catastrophic nuclear war. At the same time, the United States maintained a large and expensive military presence in Europe, because this was widely agreed to be necessary to protect American interests by deterring a Soviet attack.

The limits that govern American foreign policy are not formally encoded in a foreign policy charter and are seldom even set out explicitly. They are more like

customs in small-scale societies or good manners in
larger ones: they are tacitly, but widely, understood.
Prudent people who wish to be considered members
in good standing of the foreign policy establishment
take care not to violate these limits.

In the United States, issues of foreign policy, like
their domestic counterparts, are energetically debated. Sharply different preferences are regularly ad-
vocated for advancing American interests in the
Middle East, for example, or on the subject of nuclear
proliferation. Those debates, however, take place
within these limits. Just as the rules of baseball determine what players can and cannot do on the baseball
diamond in pursuit of victory for their teams, so the
tacit boundaries of American foreign policy determine
what may be legitimately proposed and carried out to
further the national interests of the United States.

The economic crisis of 2008 and especially the gar-
gantuan economic obligations that will confront the
country in its wake will redraw those boundaries in
two closely related ways. First, the limits of the possible for foreign policy will be narrower than they
have been for many decades. The government will
still have an allowance to spend on foreign affairs, but
because competing costs will rise it will be smaller
than in the past. Evidence of the narrowing of the

publicly permitted scope for foreign policy appeared in a poll conducted by the Pew Research Center and the Council on Foreign Relations in the latter half of 2009. It found that a higher proportion of Americans agreed that the United States should "mind its own business internationally"—49 percent—than at any time since the Gallup survey had first asked this particular question, in 1964. Only 44 percent of the respondents disagreed with this sentiment. Not coincidentally, the proportion of Americans who considered the national debt the country's most serious problem rose sharply, according to other polls.

Second, the limits that constrain the government in its external initiatives will be drawn less on the basis of what the world requires and more by considering what the United States can—and cannot—afford. In an era in which fewer resources will be available for everything, it is certain that fewer will be available for foreign policy. When working Americans are paying more than in the past to support their fellow citizens who have retired, and retirees are receiving fewer benefits from the government than they were promised, neither group will be eager to offer generous support to overseas ventures.

To be sure, a tug-of-war between domestic and foreign obligations is nothing new. Since the end of the nineteenth century, after all, the trade-off between international and domestic expenditures—between guns and butter—has been part of American political debate. Critics of foreign policy of all types, but especially of wars, have decried the diversion of resources to foreign adventures that they believed could better have been spent at home. Moreover, American foreign policy has always operated within limits of some kind. The country has never been free to do anything it wished, nor has the government ever been free to carry out any foreign policy it chose, regardless of cost.

Yet for the foreign policy of the United States for almost seven decades beginning with World War II, and in contrast to the experience of almost every country throughout history, freedom of maneuver rather than constraints on action was the norm. In foreign affairs as in economic policy, the watchword was "more." That era has ended. The defining fact of foreign policy in the second decade of the twenty-first century and beyond will be "less."

CHAPTER TWO
———

THE NOVELTY OF SCARCITY

THE ARC OF AMERICAN FOREIGN POLICY

While varied and complicated, the history of American foreign policy since the founding of the country displays one consistent theme: expansion. During the first century of that history, the thirteen original colonies expanded across North America to the Pacific Ocean, and even beyond, to the Hawaiian Islands. In 1898 the United States acquired a modest version of the existing European overseas empires by defeating Spain and taking possession of the Philippines.

In 1917, with the largest economy on the planet, the country entered World War I and helped tip the balance in favor of its allies, Great Britain and France. After the war, while withdrawing from the military affairs of the European continent, the United States took part in the European economic diplomacy of the 1920s. By the eve of the Second World War it had established itself as a significant participant in international affairs. It was World War II, however—which began for the United States with an attack by Japan on its naval base at Pearl Harbor on December 7, 1941—that inaugurated the era of foreign policy that featured an ongoing military presence and nonstop diplomatic activity around the world, along with a negligible role for considerations of cost. Almost seventy years later, cost is set to become far more important.

For the countries of Europe, the Second World War repeated, and in some ways continued, the first one. The United States, however, had markedly different experiences in the two world wars. America entered World War II far earlier in the course of the fighting than it had World War I: the cost to the country of the second war was therefore considerably higher. American military forces had a much greater impact on the outcome of the second than on the first war. And for the United States, World War II became a global enterprise as World War I had not been: the

American military took part in the fighting in the European, Asian, Atlantic, Pacific, and North African theaters.

The demands of foreign policy achieved a higher priority in the United States between 1941 and 1945 than before or since. The nation fielded armed forces totaling more than 4 million men and women. A very large proportion of those who did not serve in uniform, women as well as men, worked in industries that produced arms and supplies for the military. The entire society was mobilized to wage an immense war, one in which all the countries involved made use of every resource, every weapon, and every tactic at their disposal in pursuit of victory.

The end of World War II in 1945 might have been expected to bring about a sharp reversal of the expansive reach of American international initiatives. Instead, the aftermath of the Second World War witnessed the establishment of a pattern for American foreign policy that endured for almost seven decades.

To be sure, considerable demobilization did take place once Germany and Japan had surrendered: the armed forces shrank, as did the proportion of the nation's total production devoted to defense. The end of World War II surely would have begun a long-term contraction in the scope of American foreign policy had it not been for the almost immediate onset of a different kind of conflict, one that pervaded American public life for the next four decades: the Cold War.

The Cold War lasted so much longer than World War II—from the mid-1940s to the end of the 1980s—that it is better understood as an era than as an event. Unlike World War II, it did not have a clear beginning; there was no equivalent of the Japanese attack on Pearl Harbor. Instead, between the end of World War II and the outbreak of the Korean War in 1950, a series of political events in Europe turned the United States and the Soviet Union, which had been wartime allies against Nazi Germany, into full-fledged global rivals.

Unlike World War II, waging the Cold War was, for most Americans, consistent with a normal civilian existence, including a steady rate of economic growth that helped to support the military spending and diplomatic initiatives of the period. Unlike World War II, the level of national effort that the Cold War required varied over time. A telling measure of that effort, the American defense budget, regularly rose and fell as percentage of the total national economy.

Still, American foreign policy during the Cold War decades operated on the same global scale as in

World War II. The United States again confronted a powerful adversary, one capable, if unchecked, of dominating the international system. That confrontation stood at the center of the nation's relations with all other countries: every American foreign policy was connected to it in some way. And almost everything that happened around the world had, or was thought to have, the potential to tilt the balance of power in favor of either the Soviet Union or the United States. An election in Europe, a civil war in Africa, a coup in Latin America were all seen as affecting the security of the United States, so the American government had to have the reach and the resources not only to monitor these events but also, if necessary, to influence them.

For this very broad purpose, the United States retained the institutions that it had built during World War II: a substantial standing military force, a large diplomatic corps, several agencies for gathering intelligence abroad, and a far-flung system of alliances, with American military bases located in the allied countries.

Unlike World War II, the two major antagonists of the Cold War never fought each other directly. Each was deterred by the other's stockpile of nuclear weapons, but the United States did wage two major wars against Soviet allies in Korea and Vietnam. Throughout the Cold War, moreover, as during World War II, Americans believed that they faced a threat from abroad that required vigilance and sacrifice. They believed, as well, that to protect themselves and to assure the nation's interests a foreign policy as expansive, although not as expensive, as the one the United States had pursued during World War II was necessary. For more than four decades, the United States conducted its foreign policy on a wartime footing.

Eventually the Cold War, too, came to an end. When it did, Soviet armed forces withdrew from positions as far west as the middle of Germany that they had occupied during the course of World War II, positions that Americans had considered threatening to Western Europe and therefore to the United States as well. At the end of 1991 the Soviet Union itself, the great communist multinational empire of Eurasia that the Bolshevik Party had assembled after seizing power in Russia in 1917, collapsed entirely. The threat it had presented disappeared. Yet even in the absence of a major threat—indeed, in no small part *because* of the absence of such a threat—the United States sustained, for the next two decades, a foreign policy with the same extensive geographic reach and the same institutions of foreign policy as it had had during World War II and the Cold War. Post–Cold War American foreign policy prominently included, in fact, aspirations for promoting change in other countries that in some ways were even more ambitious than its goals during World War II and the Cold War.

American foreign policy after the Cold War divides into two parts. During most of the first, which ran from the collapse of the Soviet Union itself in 1991 to the attacks of September 11, 2001, Bill Clinton was president. For all of the second, from the moment of those attacks to the financial collapse of September 15, 2008, George W. Bush presided over the nation's foreign policy. In neither period did the United States have to confront a powerful, hostile, aggressive adversary like Nazi Germany or the Soviet Union. The terrorist network against which the Bush administration declared war, although certainly dangerous, had nothing remotely like the capabilities of the nation's principal adversaries between 1941 and 1991. Accordingly, the country spent less on the most expensive feature of foreign policy, the armed forces. As a percentage of the American gross domestic product, the defense budget fell by almost half.

Despite this decrease in military spending, the United States continued to conduct a foreign policy of global scope using the institutions of the Cold War era. Its defense budget, although reduced from Cold War levels, far surpassed that of any other country; indeed, at one point it was larger, in dollar terms, than those of the next fourteen highest national defense budgets combined.

While spending less on its armed forces, moreover, the United States used them more frequently after the end of the Cold War than before. The Clinton administration took military action in Somalia, Haiti, Bosnia, and Kosovo. In the wake of the terrorist attacks on New York and Washington, the Bush administration sent to Afghanistan and Iraq expeditionary forces that overturned anti-American governments and stayed to try to pacify the countries.

During the Cold War, the American government's use of its armed forces was kept in check by the possibility that they would come into direct contact with those of the Soviet Union and the near certainty that, even short of this, the Soviet Union and other communist countries would make any war expensive for the United States by supporting America's adversaries, which is what happened in Korea and Vietnam. Military intervention became cheaper and less dangerous with the passing of the Cold War, and with the passing of the Cold War the United States intervened more frequently.

Between 1941 and 1991, whenever America deployed its armed forces abroad prepared to fight or actually sent them into battle, the purpose was to defend itself against foreign threats. Military intervention in the post–Cold War decades had different purposes. The Clinton administration dispatched troops to rescue people in danger, usually from the assaults of those who governed them. The practice became known as "humanitarian intervention:" rather than protecting Americans from military forces controlled by other governments, the United States undertook to protect non-Americans from their own governments. This was a new development: few countries have ever been powerful enough (and even fewer generous enough) to be able, let alone willing, to use their armed forces in ways that brought them no direct benefit.

In sending troops to Afghanistan in 2001, the Bush administration was fighting the most familiar kind of war, and the one with the strongest support in international law. It was responding to an attack, and thus acting in self-defense. The campaign to remove the Iraqi dictator Saddam Hussein from power in 2003, however, had as its justification the prospect that, if left in charge of the country, he was likely to act in ways that jeopardized major American interests. The United States thus waged a preventive war against Iraq, an unfamiliar kind of war in American history and a kind of war that international law does not allow. The Bush administration announced as goals for the protracted and bloody military deployments in Afghanistan and Iraq not only to defeat anti-American forces but also to bring democratic government to the two countries. Neither of them had such a government at the time of the American intervention or indeed had ever had one.

These post–Cold War goals of American military intervention were more ambitious, complicated, and, as it turned out, difficult to achieve than the older, more familiar, and relatively straightforward aims, which had animated foreign policy before 1991, of defending the country and its vital interests. Rather than leading to a contraction of the nation's foreign policy, the end of the Cold War had the opposite impact. The United States had always sympathized with foreigners oppressed by their governments and had aspired to spread the blessings of democracy beyond North America. But it was only with the apparent end of the Cold War, and with it the apparent end of making the protection of the United States from mortal threats the overriding goal of American foreign policy, that these sympathies and aspirations could achieve the prominence, and claim the resources, that they did during the Clinton and George W. Bush presidencies.

From 1941 to 1991 and then from 1991 to 2008, the United States carried out the same kind of foreign policy, but for opposite reasons. In the first period, such a policy was necessary to meet the threat the country faced; in the second, it was possible precisely because there was no such threat. In the first era, the nation's security required that it mount the foreign policy it did; in the second, without a comparable threat but also without serious economic constraints, it could comfortably afford such a foreign policy. In the first, the price of not being active all over the world seemed unacceptably high; in the second, the economic, political, and military costs of such activism seemed, for the most part, acceptably low. For five decades, in conducting its foreign policy, the United States operated with the mind-set of a doctor, doing whatever was necessary to safeguard the patient—that is, itself. For the next two decades it assumed the role of the philanthropist, investing its large surplus of power and wealth in worthy causes all over the planet.

The financial and economic circumstances of the second decade of the twenty-first century will not by themselves re-create the kind of external military and political danger that necessitated the global role of the first era. They will, however, put an end to the condition that made such policies possible in the second. The reversal of the expansive American foreign policy that seemed imminent at the end of World War II, and again at the end of the Cold War, has finally arrived.

THE LIMITS OF AMERICAN DECLINE

Where will the consequences of the great reversal in American foreign policy be felt? While they will certainly be felt in some ways by the people who have ultimate sway over that policy—the American public—the most important impact of these new limits will come not in the United States but in other countries. The rest of the world will change because American foreign policy has played such a large role in the rest of the world.

As for the nature of that change, two different perspectives are likely to become the main frameworks for understanding the consequences of the constraints that the country's domestic economic challenges will impose on its foreign policy. One is the perspective of the historian, which places the United States and its foreign policy in a wider historical context and thus permits a comparison with the great powers of the past. The other perspective might be called the anti-American approach to the interpretation of American foreign policy: its premise is a negative judgment on the foreign relations of the United States. Each, however, misleads more than it illuminates because neither proceeds from an accurate understanding of the unique features of America's global role in the twenty-first century.

A retrenchment in its international activities is unusual for the United States, but the decline in the international reach and ambitions of powerful countries is anything but unusual in the history of international relations. To the contrary, it is the norm. One of the principal themes of international history—perhaps its major theme—is expressed by the title of a book on the subject by the eminent historian Paul Kennedy: *The Rise and Fall of the Great Powers*. Like flowers, powerful countries have tended, over the centuries, to bloom and then to fade.

In Kennedy's telling, the great powers of the past five centuries have regularly suffered from "imperial overstretch." The rising cost of maintaining an armed presence beyond their borders weakens them internally to the point that they suffer defeat in a major war and a consequent demotion in the international hierarchy. To be sure, in the age of nuclear weapons a great, hierarchy-changing war is unlikely, and the expenses that are forcing a contraction in American foreign policy come from within rather than outside the country's borders: America's problem is "entitlement overstretch."

The general pattern is, however, a familiar one, not least in the twentieth century. While the United States rose to a position of global primacy, other sovereign states declined in power and influence, with the collapse of the Soviet Union in 1991 being merely the most recent. As a result of World War I, the great land empires of Eurasia—those of the Habsburgs in Central Europe; the Ottomans in southern Europe, Anatolia, and the Middle East; and the Romanovs, which stretched from Poland to the Pacific Ocean, all of them long established and all of them defeated in the war—ceased to exist. World War II so weakened Great Britain and France, even though the British were part of the winning coalition, that over the next decade they both liquidated their overseas empires. The British empire had been the largest in the world, the one on which the sun never set. As Britain declined, the United States assumed some of its global responsibilities.

The United States of the twenty-first century, however, even with the economic pressure that the 2008 financial crisis has produced, its rising debt burden, and its unfunded entitlement obligations, differs from the declining powers of the twentieth century, and the centuries before, in two important ways. First, the American decline will not be nearly as steep as the previous ones. The American empire will not disappear, as did the empires of the twentieth century, because the United States does not have an empire. The American economy will remain the largest one on the planet for some time to come, and American military forces, for the foreseeable future, will be the world's most powerful.

The economic shocks constraining American power have affected other countries as well, which means that, even with the economic challenges it faces, the American margin of superiority in usable power over many other countries will not diminish. That fact is connected to a second key difference between the twenty-first-century United States and other countries whose power has waned. No other country will, in the foreseeable future, rise to challenge America's global role, let alone supplant it as the most powerful member of the international system.

Neither of the two candidates usually cited as challengers and successors to the United States will attain such a status in the near future, if ever. The countries of Europe are wealthy and have both experience as global powers in the past and aspirations—at least rhetorically—to resume that role in the future. In part in hopes of resuming it, they have banded together to form the twenty-seven-member European Union (EU), with a population of 491 million and an output of $14 trillion. (The comparable figures for the United States are 300 million and $14 trillion.) Anticipating the often-predicted emergence of Europe as a twenty-first-century powerhouse in international affairs comparable to the United States, however, resembles the plot of the Samuel Beckett play *Waiting for Godot.*

Godot never arrives and the European superpower will not arrive either. For one thing, the demographic pressures that make American entitlement programs so burdensome will weigh even more heavily on Europe. Birthrates there are lower than in the United States, so unlike in the United States, the populations of many European countries will actually shrink. With retirement benefits generally higher, European workers will have to pay more to support the nonworking populations, leaving fewer resources for other endeavors and contributing to slower economic growth than in the United States. More important, the EU has proven itself unable to act as a single unit in political and military affairs. Even if the EU could somehow manage to forge a consensus on security issues, an achievement that has thus far eluded it, it has very little usable military force to back up whatever policies it might choose to adopt.

A more plausible candidate to challenge and ultimately surpass the United States is China. It has the world's largest population and fastest-growing economy. At some point in the twenty-first century it will almost certainly overtake the United States as the possessor of the world's largest economy measured by total production. Although not necessarily in straightforward fashion, economic growth does enhance a country's international influence, so China's influence is destined to grow, perhaps rapidly, in the decades ahead.

Yet in the decades ahead China will remain a poor country as measured by per capita income. Whatever regime governs the country will have as its highest priority improving the fortunes of the hundreds of millions of Chinese who will remain poor, which will direct the country's attention and energies inward. China's population will also grow older, although later in the century than Europe's, as the result of the one-child-per-couple policy the government imposed on

Chinese families beginning in the 1970s. China, too, will have to support an expanding number of retired workers with a shrinking pool of people active in the workforce. This will constrain China's international activities in the middle years of the century just as an aging population and its fiscal consequences will restrict American foreign policies in its second decade and beyond. China's international influence will surely continue to grow, above all in East Asia, but not so rapidly as to displace that of the United States.

While the United States will have fewer resources for foreign policy, therefore, others will not necessarily have more. America will be able to do less internationally compared to what it has done in the past, but this does not mean that the international efforts of others will rise in proportion to the American decline. What the world's strongest power faces in conduct of its foreign policy is not only (and perhaps not mainly) weakness in relation to others but also, where usable foreign policy resources are concerned, scarcity.

The prospect of scarcity in disposable American power will come as welcome news to the anti-Americans, in whose view American power is the principal source of the world's troubles. Evidence of this sentiment can be found all over the world, including in the United States. The anti-Americanism that is manifested in opinion polls, demonstrations, political speeches, and private conversations has a variety of sources.

In the Arab Middle East, for example, oppressive dictatorships use the United States as a scapegoat for their own failures, and hostility to America is virtually the only political view, aside from support for the regimes, that governments permit to be publicly expressed. The administration of George W. Bush attracted special opprobrium in Western Europe because the core principles of his Republican Party—assertive nationalism, social conservatism, and a hostility toward taxation—are not widely shared on the Continent and thus made his government seem alien and vaguely menacing.

Anti-Americans believe that the less powerful the United States is, the better off they, their countries, and the rest of the world will be. With the exception of the terrorist devotees of fundamentalist Islam and the leaders of North Korea, Cuba, Venezuela, and a handful of other countries, however, those who believe this are wrong. American power confers benefits on most inhabitants of the planet, even on many who dislike it and some who actively oppose it, because the United States plays a major, constructive, and historically unprecedented role in the world.

The World's Government

When societies become sufficiently complex, and its members closely enough connected with one another, they require a government to set rules, keep order, and support their various transactions. The small bands of hunter-gatherers of prehistory did not need formal government. The settled agricultural communities of antiquity and the premodern era, and of course the great urban civilizations of today, emphatically do need it.

So it has been with the contemporary society of sovereign states. As cross-border trade and investment have grown, and as the march of technology has produced ever more powerful weapons that have vastly expanded the destructive potential of warfare, the world has come to need governance. Much of the governance that the world has comes from the United States. In the twenty-first century the United States provides to the world some of the services that governments within countries furnish to the societies they govern.

The first duty of government is to keep order. American security commitments in Europe and East Asia, the two most economically productive and heavily armed parts of the world outside North America, and the American military forces deployed there, help to keep order by providing reassurance in both regions. Reassurance is the policy of instilling confidence in countries that they are not in imminent danger, that sources of insecurity will not suddenly materialize, and that they can therefore conduct their relations with other countries without fear. The United States provides reassurance by serving as a buffer between and among countries that are not actively hostile to one another but that harbor fears that hostility might someday arise. Effective reassurance, like good fences in the Robert Frost poem, makes good neighbors.

Specifically, the American security role in Europe reassures the Western Europeans that if Russia should attempt to intimidate them, the United States will protect them as it did during the Cold War. At the same time, the American military presence in Europe and the enduring alliance with Germany reassure Russia that Germany itself, which invaded Russia twice in the first half of the twentieth century, will not become a major, aggressive military power again. The similar American role in Asia reassures the countries of the region that they have a means of counterbalancing China, while reassuring China that Japan, like Germany an American ally and one that invaded and occupied the Chinese mainland in the twentieth century, will not reprise its past pattern of conquest. The

American military presence in both regions, although reduced from its Cold War levels, enables the countries in each to feel that the region is safe and that they can behave accordingly, just as a policeman on patrol imparts a sense of safety to a neighborhood.

The United States has also taken the lead in trying to prevent what is, by common consent, the most urgent threat to international security in the twenty-first century: the spread of nuclear weapons to governments, or non-governmental groups such as terrorist organizations, that would wield them in dangerous ways or even actually use them. The Non-Proliferation Treaty (NPT) of 1968 enshrines the global norm against the spread of nuclear weapons, but the treaty does not provide the means to enforce this norm. American political leadership, American surveillance techniques and intelligence-gathering organizations, and sometimes American military power have done more to keep these weapons from spreading than the efforts of any other country. The military forces that provide reassurance also aid the cause of nonproliferation: without the assurance of American protection if it should be needed, Germany and Japan might well conclude that, to deal on an equal basis with their nuclear-armed neighbors Russia and China, they themselves need nuclear weapons.

American military forces also provide important services to the global economy. In national economies people have the confidence to trade and invest freely because they know that the government stands ready to step in and enforce the contracts they make if this should be necessary. Governments punish default and theft. American military forces perform a version of this function for cross-border economic transactions: the U.S. Navy patrols and safeguards the world's most important trade routes, the Atlantic and Pacific oceans.

Governments also supply electricity and water to their citizens. The international equivalent of these public utilities, necessary for the smooth functioning of everyday life in much of the world, is a reliable supply of oil. American diplomacy and the American armed forces have guaranteed such a supply by ensuring a measure of political stability in the region with the planet's largest reserves of readily accessible petroleum—the Persian Gulf—and by safeguarding the sea lanes along which the oil moves from producers to consumers.

Governments routinely supply the currency that their citizens use, and for international transactions the most frequently used currency comes from the United States—the American dollar. Because it is so frequently employed, the dollar is also the world's most widely held reserve currency, reserves being liquid resources that countries keep on hand to pay their foreign debts and foster confidence in their own national currencies.

In times of economic downturn, finally, twenty-first-century economic orthodoxy, based on the writings of John Maynard Keynes, teaches that the government must stimulate or provide directly the consumption that ordinarily comes from firms and individuals. Here, too, the United States has made a quasi-governmental contribution to the international economy. Especially in the last decade of the twentieth century and for most of the first decade of the twenty-first, the United States furnished a very large proportion of the world's total consumption, sustaining economic growth in parts of the planet far from North America. This is a role that the financial crisis of 2008 brought to an abrupt end, plunging the world into a deep recession.

No good deed, an old saying has it, goes unpunished. The American role as the world's government partly bears this out: the governmental services that it provides qualify as good deeds in that they confer benefits on others who do not have to pay for them. In providing them, however, the United States does not act in an entirely selfless fashion: tranquillity in East Asia and Europe, where the United States fought several wars in the course of the twentieth century, and an open international economic order in which the United States can import and export freely and invest and receive capital across national borders, bring considerable benefits to America as well. And while anti-Americanism can be unpleasant, it is generally not painful for the United States. The good deeds of global governance are not so much punished as unappreciated. For this there are several reasons.

First and foremost, the United States does not look, or in every way act, like the world's government. It does not have, nor, despite what critics of American foreign policy sometimes claim, does it seek to have on a global scale the defining property of an ordinary state within its domain—a monopoly of force. Moreover, the most important governmental functions that the United States carries out for the rest of the world—reassurance and enforcement—are not only not readily recognizable, they are all but invisible. They depend simply on the presence of American forces.

Americans themselves were never asked to provide governance to the rest of the world and do not think of themselves as doing so. For the most part, the global services they underwrite represent the continuation, in the twenty-first century, of policies adopted during the Cold War as part of the political, military, economic, and ideological competition with the Soviet Union and international communism.

Nor do the citizens of other countries see America as providing a de facto world government. They would certainly be loath to concede to the United States the special status that explicit recognition of what it does globally would bring. The governments of other countries understand far better than their citizens what American military and economic power does for the rest of the world. They vote, in effect, with their money in favor of American-supplied global governance by holding dollars, and in some cases with their sovereign territory by permitting the (occasionally secret) installation of American military facilities in Europe, Asia, and the Middle East. By one estimate, at the outset of the twenty-first century American special forces operated in no fewer than 125 countries. These other countries seldom acknowledge what they owe to the United States, however, no doubt in part to avoid encouraging the idea that since American foreign policies do so much to make them secure and prosperous, they should contribute far more than they do to pay for these policies.

While not volunteering to support the governmental services the United States furnishes, the governments of every other major country have done nothing to oppose America's global role. The absence of active opposition demonstrates that, whatever they say or refrain from saying publicly, other governments recognize privately how important American foreign policy is for their own countries' well-being. Historically, when a single country became as powerful as the United States came to be after the Soviet Union collapsed, other powers banded together to restrain it. In the wake of the Cold War no such thing has happened, and the absence of such an anti-American coalition testifies eloquently to the American role as the world's government.

The term that hints at the special character of America's role in the world that has found its way into common usage, at least among other governments and within the ranks of the American foreign policy community, is "leadership." Although not recognized as such by those who use the term, in this context "leadership" is a synonym for "government." It is this role, by whatever name it is known, that the coming economic challenges will place at risk.

Because what the United States does beyond its borders is, on the whole, extremely constructive, everyone, not only Americans, has a great deal to lose from a reduction in American power. Indeed, other countries may have more to lose from a diminished American global role than does the United States, which will remain powerful enough to protect itself in a more dangerous international order and whose economy is large enough to minimize the damage from a reduction in international trade and investment. All countries, however, the United States included, would suffer from a less stable, less prosperous international system.

The central task of American foreign policy, even as these economic challenges constrain it, is to preserve as many of the vital governmental services the United States supplies to the world as possible. The challenge for American policy in the second decade of the twenty-first century is to provide leadership on a shoestring—or at least on a much reduced budget. There are two obvious strategies for doing so.

One is to discard some responsibilities, the better to sustain others. To govern is to choose, and in its capacity as the world's government the United States will have to choose for continuation the policies that make the most important contributions to its own and the world's well-being, while discontinuing others that, however worthy, do less to promote American interests and a benign world order. The other strategy is to share the burden of furnishing global services with other countries.

The impending scarcity of foreign policy resources in the United States is, on the whole, an unfortunate development. It puts in jeopardy a variety of American-provided services that have made the world a safer and more prosperous place than it would have been without them. Scarcity does, however, have one potentially beneficial consequence. Just as losing weight can make a person healthier, the discipline that scarcity will impose can actually improve the conduct of American foreign policy by precluding the kind of errors that carelessness, itself the product of an abundance of power, produced in the first two post–Cold War decades.

CHAPTER THREE

ADAPTATION TO SCARCITY

THE SEAT BELT EFFECT

The Duchess of Windsor, distilling the lessons of a life of affluent idleness, once decreed that a person "can never be too thin or too rich." Of this widely repeated maxim someone once commented that the life of Howard Hughes, the very eccentric billionaire who starved himself to death, provided evidence to the contrary.

For the international system, the equivalent of the Duchess's rule is that a country can never have too much power; but the experience of the United States in the post–Cold War era, like the case of the late Mr. Hughes, counts as an exception. During the two decades following the collapse of communism, the United States stood at the zenith of its power, with a margin of superiority over all other countries as great as, perhaps greater than, any single country had ever enjoyed in the long history of international relations. Yet in this period the United States committed two costly, foreseeable, and avoidable foreign policy blunders.

The misguided and dangerous decision by the Clinton administration to expand the North Atlantic Treaty Organization (NATO) in the mid-1990s, over the objections of the newly non-communist Russia, and the disastrous ineptitude with which the Bush administration conducted the occupation of Iraq in 2003 and afterward, substantially weakened the American position in the world. Just as Howard Hughes's vast wealth and peculiar dietary habits, far from improving his life, actually hastened his own death, so the unprecedented strength of the United States in comparison to every other country after the end of the Cold War, far from preventing these serious foreign policy errors, actually contributed to them. With fewer resources to devote to foreign policy, America is less likely to make mistakes like these.

The two great post–Cold War mistakes followed the logic of what economists, in another context, have called the Peltzman Effect. Named for its discoverer, the University of Chicago economist Sam Peltzman, the Peltzman Effect refers to the occasional tendency of regulations that governments impose on the economy to have, perversely, the opposite of their intended effects. An often-cited example involves seat belts in automobiles, the use of which, according to some studies, actually *increases* the rate of accidents. The reason is that seat-belted drivers become more confident and less careful, and drive more recklessly. So it was with post–Cold War American foreign policy.

This does not mean that seat belts should be eliminated. Accidents that do take place—and not all are caused by the excessive confidence of the seat-belt wearer—generally have less serious consequences for those who buckle up than for those who do not. Nor will the United States or the world be better off with a less rather than a more powerful America; the contrary is true. But as with the wearing of a seat belt, overwhelming power did lead to unnecessary post–Cold War costs for the United States, and for the same reason. It bred carelessness, and carelessness led to serious mishaps in Eastern Europe and the Middle East.

In 1999, after a vigorous debate in the United States, the sixteen-nation NATO extended membership to three formerly communist-ruled Central European countries: Poland, Hungary, and the Czech Republic. In the next ten years nine other formerly communist countries joined, including Lithuania, Latvia, and Estonia, all three of which had once been part of the Soviet Union itself and shared borders with the new Russia.

NATO expansion soured relations with Russia because expansion broke the promise that Soviet leaders believed, with good reason, they had received from their Western counterparts, as the Cold War wound down, that NATO would not extend its reach into what had been communist Europe. The result was to create festering doubts in the minds of Russians about the trustworthiness of the West and particularly of the United States.

The Russians objected publicly and frequently to NATO expansion but their objections were ignored. They were ignored because the United States and its allies assumed they could afford to ignore them: Russia was too weak to stop the process. Bitter at what they saw as the exploitation of their weakness, the Russian political class and much of the Russian public turned against the United States, and opposition to American initiatives became the default position for

Russian foreign policy. This proved costly for the United States. The chances of preventing Iran from acquiring nuclear weapons, for example, a major American goal, came to depend heavily on enlisting wholehearted Russian support; and Russian assistance to the American campaign against Iranian nuclear proliferation was anything but wholehearted. Overall, the Russian resentment of and opposition to American power that NATO expansion generated resulted in the weakening of the United States.

The Russian reaction should not have come as a surprise. Few geopolitical developments have been so widely predicted. When the initial expansion was being debated, the consensus view of experts on Russia was expressed by perhaps the most eminent of them, George F. Kennan, a former diplomat, a noted historian, and one of the principal architects of the policy of containment of the Soviet Union that the United States had followed during the Cold War. In a 1997 article in *The New York Times*, Kennan called expansion "the most fateful error of American policy in the entire post–Cold War era."

The Clinton administration gave as its rationale for expansion the extension of democracy eastward. But it offered inconsistent versions of this rationale and none made sense. On some occasions Clinton administration officials described NATO membership for the formerly communist countries as a reward for becoming democracies. Why this was an appropriate basis for an invitation to join NATO was never made clear, especially since undemocratic countries during the Cold War (Greece and Turkey under military rule, for example) had been members of the alliance in good standing. On other occasions, NATO expansion was advertised by the Clinton administration as a way of promoting democracy where it had not yet fully taken hold. This made no sense because the democratic political direction of the first new members, Poland, Hungary, and the Czech Republic, was not in doubt. Moreover, if the United States had truly believed that a place in NATO would guarantee free elections and constitutional rights, the offer of membership should immediately have been extended to the largest formerly communist country, where the fate of democracy was of paramount importance and where its success still hung in the balance: Russia. Instead, the Clinton administration told the Russians that they would never be invited to join.

The Clinton administration's principal motive for expanding NATO was to make political gains in advance of the 1996 presidential election among American voters of Polish, Hungarian, and Czech heritage by promising NATO membership to the countries from which their forebears had immigrated. During the Cold War, such political benefits would have been outweighed by the risks involved in angering America's most powerful rival, the Soviet Union. But by the mid-1990s the Cold War had ended and the new Russia was far less formidable than the old Soviet Union. The risks seemed to Bill Clinton and his colleagues—wrongly, as it turned out—to be negligible. The administration felt free to ignore Russia's wishes. With the geopolitical equivalent of a seat belt—American strength and corresponding Russian weakness—seemingly securely fastened, it plowed recklessly ahead with expansion despite all the warnings it received.

NATO expansion might be imputed to the peculiar features of the administration that launched it—the all-consuming desire of the president to please every possible domestic constituency and the susceptibility of his Democratic Party to policies that appeared on their face to support American values (as distinct from the national interest). The next administration, however, with a different presidential personality and a different approach to foreign policy, fell into a similar trap. Again ignoring ample warning, the administration of George W. Bush committed a costly blunder in Iraq.

The debacle in Iraq resembled, in important ways, the misstep of NATO expansion. The resemblance strongly suggests that at the root of both was a feature of post–Cold War foreign policy that transcended partisan differences. What the two fiascoes had in common was expressed in F. Scott Fitzgerald's 1925 novel, *The Great Gatsby*, by the book's narrator, Nick Carraway, in describing the wealthy socialites Tom and Daisy Buchanan. "They were careless people. . . . They smashed up things and creatures and then re-treated back into their money or their vast careless-ness." The carelessness at the root of the foreign policy blunders was born of the remarkably favorable geopolitical circumstances in which the end of the Cold War left the United States.

Like NATO expansion, the American war in Iraq, which began with an invasion of the country in March 2003, proved costly. Seven years later more than 4,000 Americans had been killed and 30,000 had been wounded, 14,000 of them severely enough not to return to duty within seventy-two hours. The death toll of Iraqis, almost all of them civilians, was by a rough count around 100,000. The war had cost almost a trillion dollars, and by the estimate of econ-omists Linda Bilmes and Joseph Stiglitz the ultimate bill might well come to three times that amount. Iraq divided the American public more sharply than had any issue since the conflict in Vietnam a generation previously. Its unpopularity beyond America's borders cost the United States prestige and influence in the international arena.

While the decision to invade Iraq in the first place aroused controversy, and the absence of the weapons of mass destruction that the Iraqi dictator Saddam Hussein was believed to have—the possession of which had provided the principal justification for the invasion—provoked even more, the main reason the conflict turned out to be so damaging was the failure to pacify the country quickly and easily. Removing Saddam's regime, the initial goal, proved a relatively straightforward task, accomplished in three weeks with light casualties. The United States then found itself occupying the country, however, and that is where the trouble began. America's difficulties in post-Saddam Iraq were catalyzed by a series of mistakes that, like NATO expansion, were at once foreseeable, costly, and avoidable.

The American military had made no plans for the occupation. Post-conquest policies had to be improvised, leading inevitably to mistakes that careful planning might have avoided. Once it became clear that the United States would have to assume at least temporary responsibility for Iraqi stability, American officials in Washington and Baghdad had to make a series of crucial decisions concerning how to discharge that responsibility. They decided to install an American civilian administration rather than an interim Iraqi government. They decided to disband the Iraqi army. They decided to purge the government of personnel associated with Saddam Hussein's Ba'ath Party down to the middle ranks of the bureaucracy, including clerks and schoolteachers, rather than simply dismissing the top leadership.

These decisions turned out badly. They alienated important sectors of Iraqi society and inspired a deadly insurgency against the American occupation. To be sure, different decisions would also have had costs. Leaving intact the army, for example, which was controlled by the Sunni Muslims who had dominated Iraq under Saddam, might have turned the more numerous but historically oppressed Shia Muslims into active opponents of the United States.

The Bush administration, however, scarcely weighed the costs and benefits of the different options it confronted. Instead, by all accounts, it made these decisions off the cuff, haphazardly, without the kind of debate and deliberation that responsible decision-making requires. It conducted the occupation, in a word, carelessly. The carelessness extended to appointing people to staff the occupation authority on the basis of their allegiance to the conservative domestic program of the Bush administration rather than their expertise on the region: sometimes disapproval of the Supreme Court's principal abortion decision, *Roe v. Wade*, seemed to count for more than, say, mastery of the Arabic language.

The carelessness with which the occupation was initially conducted also extended, most damagingly, to include the dispatch of too few American troops for the job of keeping order in the country. The disorder that ensued—the massive looting of offices and museums after the fall of Saddam, the attacks on American and Shia targets, the growth of sectarian militias, the flourishing of terrorist groups—and the harsh American tactics in response, made the American occupation unpopular within the United States and notorious elsewhere.

Just as the Clinton administration had ostensible reasons for expanding NATO to Russia's doorstep, so the Bush administration had its reasons for believing that the occupation of Iraq would be easy and require no special preparation. Some Bush administration officials thought that the liberation of Eastern Europe from communism in 1989, when most of the formerly communist countries made relatively smooth transitions to free-market economies and democratic political systems, offered a useful precedent for the liberation of Iraq. Others based what turned out to be their excessive confidence on what in 2003 seemed the easy and inexpensive eviction of the terrorism-sponsoring Taliban regime from Afghanistan two years before and its replacement with a far friendlier and less brutal Afghan government.

As it happened, Iraq had little in common with Poland, Hungary, and the Czech Republic, and the occupation of Afghanistan was to become much more difficult for the United States in subsequent years. More to the point, the Bush administration should have been aware of the difficulties and dilemmas the conquest of Iraq would present because many individuals and groups, in and out of government, spelled them out, and did so both publicly and privately before the war began. In particular, General Eric Shinseki, the chief of staff of the army, warned that several hundred thousand troops—far more than the number actually sent—would be needed to pacify Iraq once Saddam had been overthrown. Seized by the overconfidence of the seat-belt wearer, however, the administration General Shinseki served ignored him, to the detriment of its own domestic political fortunes and the strength and global standing of the United States.

The immediate costs of Iraq, in lives and money, were higher and more palpable than the costs of NATO expansion. But someday Iraq will recede from a prominent place in the national life of the United States, just as has Vietnam, a country as important and controversial forty years earlier as Iraq was in 2009. Moreover, the American efforts in Iraq might someday come to be considered successful, if the country should evolve over the years into a stable, tolerant place with, ultimately, a democratic form of government.

NATO expansion did less damage to the United States in the short term. Unlike the invasion of Iraq, however, it has no prospect of ever providing offsetting benefits. Moreover, whereas the Iraq war will be seen in retrospect as a clumsy, unduly expensive solution to a real problem—the threat that Saddam posed—NATO expansion actually created a problem where none had existed, and that problem—the alienation of Russia—will weigh heavily on American foreign policy and international relations as far into the future as the practiced eye can see.

Whatever the balance of damage inflicted between the two episodes turns out to be, their common underlying cause—the huge disparity between the power of the United States and that of all other countries, and the carelessness to which that disparity gave rise—is becoming inoperative. The collapse of Lehman Brothers and the economic developments that have followed and will follow have, to mix a metaphor, removed the seat belts from the American ship of state. Prudence, born of straitened economic conditions, will replace the carelessness that has proven so costly in Eastern Europe and the Middle East.

The new discipline will undoubtedly improve the quality of American foreign policy in some ways, but that does not mean that the more constraining conditions can be considered, on balance, advantageous. To the contrary: as the singer Sophie Tucker once put it, "I've been rich and I've been poor and rich is better." The United States has become poorer and will cut back on the resources it devotes to its external affairs. How will that affect America's global roles?

THE END OF INTERVENTION

Of the three quasi-governmental economic services the United States provides for the world—furnishing the currency most widely used as a reserve and for international transactions, acting as the largest supplier of consumer demand, and ensuring a secure framework for cross-border economic transactions—the first is almost certain to persist in some form at least for a while. This is not because other countries are entirely pleased with the privileged status of the dollar. To the contrary, that status has become the subject of criticism and resentment because it gives the United States the capacity to borrow in its own currency, making possible the large American deficits. In addition, the special role of the dollar helped attract funds to the United States that in turn helped inflate its domestic housing bubble, the bursting of which threatened the integrity of the global financial system and plunged the world into a steep economic downturn.

If the American government should decide to cope with the huge debt it has accumulated by printing money to pay it, sending inflation soaring and destroying much of the value of the dollars other countries hold, the world might well cease to use the American currency as a store of value and a medium of exchange. Short of that, however, the dollar will likely retain its central role in international monetary affairs because the alternatives are even less satisfactory.

For example, the world will not accept as its principal form of money a currency issued by an international organization, such as the International Monetary Fund. China's currency may one day rival the dollar, but that day will not come until China's capital markets are large enough, its property rights secure enough, and its interest rates free enough of government manipulation to make citizens of other countries comfortable in holding the currency in large amounts. It would also have to become freely convertible into other currencies.

The euro, the currency used by sixteen of the twenty-seven members of the European Union, including Germany, France, and Italy, does rival the dollar: countries do hold euros as reserves and employ them in international transactions, although not on the same scale as the American currency. The euro is unlikely ever to supplant the dollar entirely, however, because of lingering worries that one or another country might someday withdraw from what is in fact a multinational currency union rather than the currency of a single country, and because the euro countries are skittish about too heavy a demand for their money, which would raise its international value and penalize the exports on which they, especially Germany, so heavily rely.

If one of the major services the United States provides to the global economy, furnishing its most important currency, will continue into the second decade of the twenty-first century, another important American economic role will not. The United States will no longer act as the world's chief consumer, furnishing an enormous and ever-expanding market for exports from East Asia and Western Europe. The American consumption binge that stoked the engines of the global economy depended on the accumulation of ever more household debt. In the wake of September 15, 2008, American consumers' spending habits changed. Saving became the order of the day. The pattern is likely to continue well into the century's second decade and perhaps beyond. Indeed, the prospects for global economic growth over the long term depend on whether, to what extent, and how rapidly other countries—especially those accustomed to running balance-of-payments surpluses such as China, Japan, and Germany—increase their own consumption to fill the gap created by post–September 15 American frugality.

As for the third major American service to the global economy, keeping order through policies that promote reassurance, nuclear nonproliferation, and freedom of the seas, all of which engender the confidence necessary for international commerce, whether these policies continue and how effective they are will depend in part on how large and capable American military forces turn out to be in an era of scarcity. That, in turn, will depend heavily on how much Americans decide to spend on defense.

One of the best-known criminals of the past century, Willie Sutton, when asked why he robbed banks, replied, "Because that's where the money is." For America's roles beyond its borders, the money—the serious money—is to be found in the defense budget, and it is therefore from defense spending, in addition to other categories of expenditure, that the post–September 15 reductions will come. During the Cold War the defense budget served as an indicator of the American public's general assessment of how dangerous a place the world was for the United States. When the danger seemed to increase, with heightened peril to American interests, defense spending rose. This occurred on several occasions: at the time of the Korean War in the early 1950s; when the Soviet Union launched the first Earth-orbiting satellite, Sputnik, in 1957; during the war in Vietnam in the 1960s; and in response to the Soviet invasion of Afghanistan in 1979. When the danger seemed to recede, defense spending—as a percentage of the federal budget and of the total national output—declined.

Without the global, mortal threat of the Soviet Union to justify it, defense spending declined sharply as a proportion of national output in the wake of the Cold War. The attacks of September 11, 2001, triggered an increase in defense expenditures, but in the following decade it never exceeded 4 percent of the

American GDP, below the average for the Cold War years. Still, 4 percent of a $14 trillion economy adds up to a lot of money. In fiscal year 2008 the defense budget was $647 billion, which was 25 percent larger in real terms than it had been in 1968, at the height of the Vietnam War—although in 2008 it was a smaller proportion of a much larger GDP. Even without a major adversary, the United States spent more on defense than most of the world's other national military budgets combined.

Downward pressure on this spending began at the outset of the Obama administration. Secretary of Defense Robert Gates, a holdover from the George W. Bush presidency, announced the termination or limitation of a number of major programs, with the promise of a more stringent approach to defense spending in the future. The partisans of such spending—the companies with contracts to produce weapon systems, the workers employed in their factories, and the members of Congress in whose districts those factories and workers were located—mobilized to resist the reductions, inaugurating what will be a protracted struggle over the size of the American defense budget.

The forces of resistance to defense cutbacks are formidable. The high-performance F-22 fighter aircraft, for example, which Gates sought to cancel after

185 had been manufactured (none was ever used in either Iraq or Afghanistan) employed a total of 25,000 people in several different states. This made it possible to generate a great deal of political support for building more of them, but the administration succeeded in getting the Congress to cap production of the airplane. Still, the first Obama defense bill included expensive projects the administration did not want but upon which powerful members of Congress insisted. And the administration itself planned a modest expansion in the size of the nation's army. Over time, however, the mounting obligations of the federal government, the strain that paying for them will impose on taxpayers, and the skepticism about federal programs other than entitlements, including defense, that rising tax bills will promote, will tilt the balance of power in this political struggle increasingly in favor of efforts to reduce the defense budget. In the future, the United States will have fewer—still, no doubt, a great many, but fewer—tanks, ships, and airplanes, and soldiers, sailors, and air crews to operate them, than it has deployed in the past.

While America will continue to supply to the world, even with these reduced forces, the services of reassurance, nonproliferation, and a secure backdrop for global commerce, one mission—a prominent and

controversial one, the one the United States undertook in Iraq and Afghanistan, among other places—
will in all likelihood be discontinued during the
course of the twenty-first century's second decade.

Between 1992 and 2003 American forces were dispatched to Somalia, Haiti, Bosnia, and Kosovo, as
well as to Afghanistan and Iraq. The American operations in these countries differed from the Cold War
interventions in Korea and Vietnam, where the
United States waged bloody, protracted campaigns
against formidable communist armies. In the post–
Cold War interventions, by contrast, American
armed forces quickly overcame the opposing armies,
but the United States then found itself having to un-
dertake an unexpected, unwanted, arduous, and frustrating task, that of creating working political
institutions in the countries it had conquered.

In none of these countries did the United States
set out to build working states: with military success,
however, came responsibility for governing the places
in question. In these places such local institutions of
governance as had once existed had collapsed and
working institutions of some kind had to be put in
place to secure the goals for which the United States
had intervened in the first place. The alternative to
state-building in Bosnia in the 1990s, for example,

was (or seemed to be) a resumption of the local wars, with the large-scale murder of civilians, that the United States had used its air force to stop. Similarly, without a prolonged American presence and an effort at state-building in Iraq, that country might have fallen into anarchy, or become a base for terrorist attacks against the West, or seen Saddam or someone like him regain power.

State-building proved difficult, frustrating, and costly everywhere it was attempted. The missing institutions, such as financial systems, judiciaries, and parliaments with political parties, could not be imported from abroad; they had to be homegrown. Such growth takes time. In the best of circumstances, working institutions require at least a generation to take root, and the places where the United States attempted state-building did not offer the best of circumstances. The skills, the values, and the historical experiences on which state institutions rest were in short supply, or nonexistent, almost everywhere that the United States intervened. This should not have been surprising. Had the conditions favorable to the growth and maintenance of banks, parliaments, and courts been present—had the state already been built—the political pathologies the United States intervened to stamp out probably would not have appeared in the first place. To make the task even more difficult and less politically palatable, these interventions cost American lives as well as money.

Despite the frustrations and the costs involved, the foreign policy community—those most knowledgeable about America's relations with other countries, including the people with direct responsibility for conducting them—came to consider such interventions to be a challenge that the United States should accept and master. They wanted to accept the challenge in part because the circumstances in which the post–Cold War interventions took place offered the opportunity to defend American values. In unstable, poorly governed (or entirely ungoverned), violent countries—"failed states," as they came to be called—values important to Americans are routinely flouted. Those unfortunate enough to reside in such places have no assurance that their lives, let alone their liberties, will be protected. Perhaps most important, communities and countries in dire need of state-building, of the kind in which the United States used military force in the first two post–Cold War decades, although distant from North America, can incubate threats to the American homeland, just as swamps breed tiny but deadly malaria-carrying mosquitoes. Terrorist cells and training camps flourish in such places. The deadliest terrorist organization, al Qaeda, established itself first in Afghanistan and then, when evicted, in the lawless northwest region of Pakistan.

From this predisposition to interventions that lead to state-building follows the idea of reconfiguring the institutions of American foreign policy to make them better suited to this task. President Bush's second secretary of state, Condoleezza Rice, called for an emphasis on "transformational diplomacy," which would use the tools of American foreign policy to transform societies in distress and in desperate need of working institutions, and the next administration took up this theme when Barack Obama entered office. At the same time, the army began to concentrate on mastering the techniques of counterinsurgency, which placed greater emphasis than the conventional arts of war on nurturing effectively civilian institutions and seemed to have made Iraq safer when applied in that country. Attending seriously to state-building, as the foreign policy community wishes, seems to require that the relevant departments of the federal government be reformed to make them competent to build institutions and train people to operate them. In this vision of foreign policy, State Department diplomats would become economists, aid workers, and public health officials, while soldiers would perform the tasks of architects, civil engineers, and teachers. Such a transformation could be seen as a large-scale, twenty-first-century version of the biblical vision of turning swords into plowshares, although at least a few swords would have to remain on hand for the purpose of keeping order.

The American public, however, does not share this vision. The public ultimately determines what the American government does and because the experience of intervention, especially in Iraq, has been, from the public's point of view, an unsatisfactory one, as well as because resources for foreign policy will be more limited in the future than in the past, the overhaul of the administrative apparatus of American foreign policy to make it an effective mechanism for state-building will not take place. Nor will the United States intervene abroad as frequently in the next two decades as it did in the past two—if indeed it intervenes at all.

The humanitarian interventions of the Clinton years were never popular with the American public as a whole. For the two military operations in the Balkans, for example, in Bosnia and Kosovo, the administration never sought, because it knew it would not receive, congressional approval. These operations were restricted to aerial bombardment so as to avoid American casualties, because the administration understood that the public would not tolerate any.

The Balkan interventions, and those in Somalia and Haiti, did not command appreciable public support because Americans, like other people, are disposed to risk the lives of their countrymen only for the sake of vital interests: that is, to prevent harm to themselves. Protecting others from harm, which is what humanitarian intervention involves, qualifies as a form of social work: admirable in principle, perhaps, but not something for which most Americans believe they should shed their soldiers' blood or spend their own tax dollars.

The public did believe that American interests were at stake in Afghanistan and Iraq. Afghanistan, after all, was the home base of the perpetrators of the attacks of September 11, which killed almost 3,000 people. In the wake of those attacks, the Bush administration persuaded the public that Saddam posed a similar, even a related, threat. The Congress did approve the Bush interventions, but those, too, lost popularity when the mission changed from removing a dangerous government to trying to keep order and construct functioning public institutions.

Avoiding military interventions and state-building is one way to lower the expense of American foreign policy. Another is to share with others the costs of the policies the country does carry out. This is particularly attractive because it offers the prospect of sustaining the existing array of policies while paying less for them. American policy-makers will therefore attempt to rely, to the extent possible, on international cooperation.

The Limits of Cooperation

In international relations, cooperation is considered the best of all possible words. Articles, books, even entire scholarly journals are devoted to trying to discover the conditions in which this practice flourishes. The cardinal sin of the Bush administration, according to some of its critics, was its failure to cooperate with other countries, opting instead for cooperation's disreputable opposite—unilateralism.

One reason for the glowing reputation of cooperation is that it connotes the absence of the worst feature of international relations: war. Countries that are cooperating are not, it is presumed, fighting each other. Another source of the bright nimbus of approbation that surrounds the idea of cooperation, especially in the United States, is that when countries cooperate they often share the costs and burdens of a common endeavor.

The decades since the end of World War II constitute the golden age of international cooperation. The fact that the wealthiest countries on the planet, those of North America, Western Europe, and Japan, confronted a common enemy—the Soviet Union and international communism—in the wake of World War II and had similar political and economic systems, gave them similar international goals. That made cooperation among them easier than had previously been the case.

Cooperation becomes institutionalized through international organizations. The post-1945 era is also, not surprisingly, the golden age of international organization. Indeed, most of the international organizations that have existed since the dawn of recorded history—certainly the vast majority of those other than temporary alliances and empires—came into existence for the first time after World War II.

In this period organizations for the promotion and regulation of cross-border economic activity in particular have proliferated. But cooperation also takes place outside the boundaries of international organizations. There is no single overarching international antiterrorism organization, for example, but national police forces and intelligence agencies have cooperated, especially since September 11, 2001, to track and neutralize the world's terrorist networks. Their record in preventing attacks is impressive, if not perfect. Still, even in its golden age, international cooperation, especially the kind that could supplement or replace the American role in the world, has severe limits.

Sovereign states do not cooperate when they do not agree on what they want. In the worst case, of course, when their goals are directly opposed, they sometimes go to war. Cooperation may also fail because, while countries do share the same goals, their preferred policies for achieving these goals differ. In the face of the global recession that began in 2008, the American government enacted a large stimulus package, which was financed by debt. The countries of the European Union, just as badly hurt by the economic downturn, spent less public money to boost private output, in part because they worried more than did the Americans about the dangers of increasing their indebtedness.

Countries can fail to cooperate as well because, while they agree on the goals they seek, their priorities among these goals differ. While all the surrounding countries disapprove of North Korea's nuclear weapons program, for example, South Korea and China have never applied maximal pressure to stop it by closing their borders to all trade with Pyongyang, because they feared the collapse of the communist regime if they did. Such a collapse would have imposed high costs on them: China would have lost a buffer state on its southern border, and South Korea would have had to accept a flood of refugees and pay heavily for the reconstruction of the North.

Neither wanted North Korea to possess nuclear weapons, or indeed had any affection for the bizarre hereditary communist regime there; but because the cost of that regime's collapse would be so high for both of them, each was willing to allow North Korea to make a bomb if that was the price they had to pay to keep the regime in place. For America, by contrast, the priorities were reversed: Washington sought above all to keep North Korea from acquiring nuclear weapons, and if the policies necessary to achieve this goal led to the end of the communist government, that was perfectly acceptable to the United States. This was so because a North Korean bomb threatened American interests in a way that the end of communist rule did not. The debris from the collapse of that regime would strike North Korea's Asian neighbors, but little if any of it seemed likely to reach North America.

Another obstacle to cooperation between and among countries, even when they have the same order of priorities, is the universal desire to minimize the expense of achieving their shared goals. Countries, like many individuals, are happy to let others pick up the check. This universal syndrome is what economists call the "free rider problem" and is the major obstacle to international cooperation in the twenty-first century. No one wants to pay to ride the bus, but if no one pays, the bus company goes bankrupt and no one rides at all.

Bus companies can deploy fare collectors to ensure that passengers pay, and governments can extract taxes from their citizens to purchase what everybody needs—such things as national defense and clean air, known as "public goods"—but for which nobody wants to pay. Since there is no world government with the power to tax, however, cooperation among countries to achieve common goals is voluntary, and there is less of it than is optimal. This is the greatest impediment the United States faces in securing the kind of cooperation that would help sustain its global roles in an era of scarcity.

The wealthy countries of Western Europe and Japan share America's basic political and economic institutions, its political and social values, and, on the whole, its preferences for the way the international system is organized and operated. They are the obvious candidates to cooperate with the United States. Indeed, since 1945 these free-market democracies have cooperated among themselves extensively. They formed the core membership of the most important and successful international organizations. The military alliances that bound them together helped to win the Cold War; the economic organizations that they established contributed to the long period of economic growth after 1945.

Yet as partners for the United States in the management of the international system in the second decade of the twenty-first century, the Europeans and Japanese have their limitations, especially when it comes to security. In the twenty-first century, the use of military force is not, to understate the matter, their strong suit. Japan's constitution places strict limits on the military operations that the country may carry out. Moreover, Japan's misdeeds during its campaign of imperial conquest in the 1930s and 1940s have not, even seven decades later, been entirely forgiven by the countries that were their victims. This makes Japan a poor candidate to supplement the American effort to police the Asia-Pacific region and elsewhere.

The countries of Europe, by contrast, have forgiven the Germans, who behaved toward them as the Japanese did in Asia, and, with Germany, have established an economic union that aspires to a global political and economic role. Although their professed ambitions have expanded as the European Union has grown larger and become more closely integrated, the European countries' individual and collective capacities to fulfill these ambitions have not. Despite Europe's size and wealth, and despite the histories of several of its countries as great military powers, it has very modest and generally declining military forces, and the Europeans are reluctant to use even the modest forces that they have.

Had the European Union's designated foreign policy spokesman, Javier Solana, gone to Washington before the launching of the Iraq war and told the Bush administration that Europe would furnish half the forces necessary to topple Saddam's regime if, but only if, the United States agreed to continue the diplomatic efforts to verify Iraq's lack of weapons of mass destruction for at least six months, it would have been impossible for American officials, no matter how determined they were to invade Iraq, to refuse. No such offer was made, of course, nor could have been made, and not only because the countries of Europe were divided over the wisdom of forcibly removing the Iraqi dictator from power. They were also incapable of providing half, or even a much smaller fraction, of the forces needed for the invasion.

While the Europeans did agree to join the American-led effort to pacify post-Taliban Afghanistan, they performed poorly there. They provided fewer troops than they promised and some of them—the Germans are a conspicuous example—imposed such stringent conditions on the operations their troops could perform as to render them all but worthless in military terms. The Western effort in Afghanistan faltered not because of a unilateral, overbearing America but rather because of a fragmented, underperforming Europe. This is likely to be the case for other such undertakings in the future. For the global services involving security that the United States has furnished to the rest of the world, cooperation with Japan and Europe promises all too little assistance.

While the world enjoys far more international cooperation in the twenty-first century than it did in the first half of the twentieth, or in any century before that, therefore, other countries are unlikely to step in to fill such gaps in global governance as the economic constraints on American foreign policy may create. The United States will still have major, in some cases exclusive, responsibility for quasi-governmental tasks that are vital to global order: providing reassurance, thwarting nuclear proliferation, and furnishing security for international economic activity; but it will have to carry out those tasks with fewer resources than in the past. Just how successful America will be will depend on how formidable are the challenges to doing so that it confronts. That, in turn, will depend on what happens beyond North America, on what other countries do, and especially on the foreign policies of the planet's two large, nuclear-armed, formerly orthodox communist countries: China and Russia.

CHAPTER FOUR

The Return of Great-Power Politics?

The Global Security Order

The international system has two overlapping parts: the global economy and the international security order. The United States plays a leading role in both. Malfunctions in either can be costly, but while a breakdown in the international economic system makes people poorer, the cost of a failure in the security order, such as the two world wars of the first half of the twentieth century, is measured in lives lost—in the case of those two conflicts, tens of millions of them.

Following September 15, 2008, the global economy experienced more turbulence and greater destruction of wealth than at any time since the Great Depression of the 1930s. The international security order, by contrast, remained largely tranquil. The post–Cold War era has in fact been calmer than any period in more than a century and a half, and in some ways calmer than at any time in the past five hundred years, because of a development virtually without historical precedent: the absence of acute military rivalries between and among the great powers. For almost all of recorded history the possibility and occasionally the fact of war dominated the policies of the strongest members of the international system, which vied for power, influence, and the control of territory. They eyed each other warily, armed themselves in anticipation of war, and sometimes fought the wars for which they were constantly preparing. The most recent chapter of this age-old story was the Cold War. Fortunately, it did not erupt into an all-out military conflict between the United States and the Soviet Union. For most of recorded history before it, however, the life of a great power was costly, dangerous, nerve-racking, and sometimes extremely bloody. That has not been the case in the twenty-first century. Since the end of World War II no great-power

war has been waged, and since the end of the Cold
War none has seemed at all likely.

The United States contributes to twenty-first-
century peace in Europe and East Asia through the
reassurance that the presence of American military
forces provides to the countries of these two regions,
but the extraordinary tranquillity of the global security order of the twenty-first century does not depend
entirely on what the United States does. The American role in Europe and East Asia supports a broader
trend: the global spread of three great ideas. The first
and most important of them is the idea of peace as
the most desirable state of international relations.
That idea is reinforced by two others: the free market
as the optimal method of organizing economic activity, and democracy as the most appropriate form of
government.

War was a normal, natural, or at least unavoidable
feature of international life for centuries. Beginning
in the second half of the twentieth century, however,
peace became the norm because war had grown so
costly. The two world wars killed tens of millions of
people and laid waste to millions of farms, factories,
and homes all over the world. At the end of World
War II the United States introduced a weapon—the
atomic bomb—capable of reducing major cities to

rubble with a single blast. In the nuclear age, war lost
its traditional function as a way of using armed force
to achieve political goals. A nuclear war of almost any
magnitude would be a senseless spasm of mass destruction for all involved.

The spread of free markets reinforced the global
commitment to peace in several ways. It offered a
new and peaceful path to wealth. Rather than con-
quering territory, which traditionally required war,
countries increased their wealth by participating in
the global marketplace. After World War II, Japan
renounced its imperial aspirations, concentrated on
international trade, and became unprecedentedly affluent. So successful were market economies in creating wealth in the second half of the past century
that the goal of enhancing the material well-being of
its citizens replaced expanding the territory it controlled as the principal objective of almost all the
world's governments. Deng Xiaoping, who led China
away from orthodox communist economics, coined
the slogan "to get rich is glorious." For most of the
world's governments in the twenty-first century it
would be more accurate to say that to get rich became
mandatory, and they understood that peace, not war,
lends itself to getting rich. Many of them prospered
by trading with countries with which they had once
engaged in bitter, brutal, bloody conflict.

Finally, the rules, habits, institutions, and values needed to operate a free-market economy, when transferred to the political sphere, tend to promote democratic politics. The popularity of free markets had a great deal to do with the flowering of democracy all over the world in the last quarter of the twentieth century, when the number of such regimes soared from thirty-five to more than one hundred. Democracies, in turn, as many studies have shown, tend to conduct less warlike foreign policies than countries with undemocratic governments. The spread of this form of government has therefore made the world of the twenty-first century more peaceful.

It is the dominance of peace, democracy, and free markets, supplemented and bolstered by the reassurance that the United States supplies, that have made the twenty-first century a peaceful period—so far. But their domination, and the global peace they underpin, are not necessarily destined to last forever; and the recent turmoil in the global economy does raise the possibility that their era of dominance will turn out to be a short one. The severe global economic downturn that the financial collapse of September 15, 2008, catalyzed threatens not only the American role in helping to maintain peace in the world but also the foundations of the stable twenty-first-century global security order itself. The international economic and security systems are not, after all, hermetically sealed off one from the other. To the contrary, each affects the other, and in the 1930s economics had a profound—and profoundly malignant—effect on politics. The crisis of the global economy led to the outbreak of the bloodiest episode in the history of international security, World War II, by bringing to power in Germany and Japan the brutal governments that started that dreadful conflict.

In the 1930s the financial crash and the high unemployment that followed all over the world discredited the shaky democratic governments in place in Germany and Japan, which fell from power. The fascist regimes that replaced them proclaimed themselves models of governance for the rest of the world and did win admirers and imitators in other countries. These regimes disdained democratic politics and practiced extensive (although not, as in the case of the Soviet Union, total) government control of economic affairs. Far from believing in peace, the two enthusiastically embraced aggressive war for the purpose of expanding the territories under their sway and subjugating—even, in some cases, attempting to exterminate—the people living there.

Japan launched a brutal campaign of conquest in China in 1931; in 1939 Germany embarked on the murderous acquisition of an Eastern European empire and in the process conquered much of Western Europe as well. The two countries forged a nominal alliance that included fascist Italy as well. During World War II they were known as the Axis powers. Japan subdued much of Asia and Germany became the master of most of Europe before the two were finally beaten, at great cost in blood and treasure, in 1945.

Could anything like the ghastly experience of the 1930s and 1940s occur in the twenty-first century? The precipitating event did, after all, repeat itself after a fashion: the economic slump that began in 2008 became, by most accounts, the most severe since the 1930s. And while Germany and Japan have long since become firmly democratic in their politics and quasi-pacifist in their foreign policies, two other countries could conceivably play the roles that the fascist powers assumed in the interwar period. Those two countries are China and Russia.

Each was, as the first decade of the new century ended, a large and militarily formidable country that had the potential to upset existing political and economic arrangements in East Asia and Europe, respectively. For much of the second half of the twentieth century the two had been governed by communist regimes that aspired to spread their form of government, by force when necessary. In the first decade of the twenty-first century neither had discarded all the trappings of its former communist identity: a communist party still ruled China, and Russians harbored nostalgia for the disbanded communist empire of the Soviet Union.

In the mid-1990s, in no small part out of resentment at the dominant global role of the United States, the two formed what they called a "strategic partnership." In that term could be heard, however faintly, the echo of the Axis alliance of World War II. China and Russia became charter members, along with five Central Asian countries, of the Shanghai Cooperation Organization, founded in 2001, one of whose apparent purposes was to offset American power. Like virtually every country, China and Russia each suffered, as had Germany and Japan in the 1930s, from the financial crisis of 2008 and the resulting economic distress.

The fascist powers were able to do enormous damage because the democracies did far too little to stop them early on. The strongest of the democracies, the United States, did the least, sending military assistance to Great Britain but refusing to engage its own forces in East Asia or Europe until Japan attacked the American naval base at Pearl Harbor on December 7, 1941, and Hitler's Germany followed with a declaration of war on the United States.

In the earlier period the United States was predisposed to stand aloof from the geopolitics of East Asia and Europe by a national tradition that dated back to the warning of its first president, George Washington, against becoming entangled in the affairs of other (and in the eighteenth century much stronger) countries. In the twenty-first century that tradition has long since been set aside, but the economic constraints under which the United States will have to operate will affect its responses to whatever challenges to the East Asian and European security arrangements China and Russia may choose to mount. On the spectrum of such challenges an assault on the scale of the ones fascist Germany and Japan launched counts as the worst case: a United States limited in its capacity to meet such a challenge would make it worse still.

Fortunately, the worst case is an unlikely one. There is little prospect that China and Russia will drag the world back to the 1930s. The economic downturn of 2008 and beyond, although serious, does not seem destined to cause economic distress to the devastating extent that the Great Depression did, and thus will not create a breeding ground for a latter-day version of fascism. China and Russia, while in important ways dissatisfied with the existing order of power and authority in the international system, will not adopt murderous, racist ideologies like the ones that motivated imperial Japan and Nazi Germany. Except among radical Islamists, such ideas have been pushed beyond the boundary of acceptability since 1945.

Nor, while they insist that their countries will not and should not conform to the democratic political standards of the West, does either China or Russia hold itself out as a distinct, non-Western model for other countries to imitate, as the Soviet Union and Nazi Germany did. China has enjoyed great economic success and other countries may well wish to follow the Chinese example, but if they do, they will not be breaking with the prevailing economic norms of the West. To the contrary, they will be carrying out the most orthodox of free-market policies: keeping their economies open to the world, building infrastructure, maintaining a stable price level, and practicing fiscal responsibility. These are policies that Western governments and international financial institutions routinely commend to one and all.

Nor is it probable that China and Russia will join together in a coordinated campaign to overturn the international status quo. Indeed, during World War II the Axis powers, despite their proclamations of solidarity, did almost nothing jointly. Similarly, despite the rhetoric of partnership and their common membership in the Shanghai Cooperation Organization, actual Sino-Russian cooperation has strict limits. In fact, each is wary of the other. Russia, in particular, regards China, with its far larger population and more dynamic economy, as a long-term threat.

All apart from the political and economic currents shaping Chinese and Russian affairs, finally, it remains true in the twenty-first century, as in the twentieth, that international economic integration, of the sort that the fascist powers spurned, is the surest route to wealth. This is the case for China and Russia as much as, if not more than, other countries, and a war of the kind that Germany and Japan once eagerly prosecuted, far from enhancing the wealth of those who waged it, would bring ruinous destruction to all its participants.

The unlikelihood of a full recurrence of all the horrors of the 1930s and 1940s does not, however, mean that the global security order is certain to remain entirely free from threats of war in the years ahead. Avoiding the worst of all possible futures does not guarantee the best of them. Even if China and Russia do not unleash murderous campaigns of conquest, this does not mean that each will settle comfortably into a twenty-first-century routine as a staunch supporter of the post–Cold War security and economic orders. Each has grievances, actual and potential, against the existing order of things. The extent to which either or both choose to act on these grievances will matter a great deal. Those choices, in turn, will depend in part on the strength of the American position in their respective regions, East Asia and Europe; and the economic constraints on the United States will weaken that position in both places.

CHINA

China is the obvious candidate to disrupt the twenty-first-century international order. As the most populous country on the planet and with the highest rate of economic growth, sustained over three decades, of any of the world's almost two hundred sovereign states, its impact on international affairs is large and destined to grow larger. Indeed, by the time of the global economic disruption of 2008 China had become so important economically as to prompt suggestions that a special Sino-American forum—a "G-2"—be established to cope with the crisis.

China's long history of cultural and political primacy in East Asia gives its people another reason to expect to play a major role in the affairs of their region and the international system as a whole. The country's experience of decline, and with it domination, humiliation, and exploitation by foreigners in the nineteenth and twentieth centuries—the official version of Chinese history that the communist government constantly emphasizes—gives its people reason to resent existing international arrangements, which they had virtually no say in devising. China therefore has both the means and the motive to act as what students of international relations call a "revisionist power," seeking to undermine the world's political and economic status quo and replace it with institutions and practices more favorable to itself.

For this there is a historical precedent, and not a happy one. At the beginning of the twentieth century Germany, like China at the outset of the twenty-first, was a rapidly rising power. The Germans came to resent the distribution of power and influence among the great powers, including the way colonial territory was allocated. As a latecomer to the upper echelon of international politics, having been unified only in 1871, Germany had not been in a position to take a major part in the nineteenth-century acquisition of overseas empires by the strongest European countries. While maintaining an adversarial relationship with France, from which their army had captured the province of Alsace-Lorraine in the Franco-Prussian War of 1870–1871, the Germans drifted into opposition, as well, to Great Britain, in some ways the leading European power as the one with the largest empire and strongest navy.

The result of the Franco-German and Anglo-German rivalries was World War I, which began, according to one not entirely facetious description, because Great Britain owned the world and Germany wanted it. The growth of China's power, its historically based aspiration for wider international prerogatives, and what some students of international politics regard as the inevitable drive by every sovereign state to maximize its own international standing at the expense of the power and privileges of other countries have combined in the twenty-first century to create the potential, if not necessarily for World War III, then at least for a robust challenge to the security of East Asia and therefore to the economically constrained guardian of stability in the region, the United States. China might, for example, seek a reduction in the American military presence or the operations of the American forces, or demand the redrawing of maritime borders, or insist on political and economic concessions from neighboring countries. It might even attack Taiwan, the island off its coast over which it claims sovereignty.

China's official rhetoric is designed to give the opposite impression of its aspirations, to soothe the anxieties that its growing strength provokes. The country is dedicated, its leaders proclaim, to a "peaceful rise" in the international system. This implies, to be sure, an ascent, but one that will not threaten others' interests and will contribute to what the Chinese government envisions as a "harmonious world." China's actual policies, however, are not quite so straightforwardly accommodating.

While not devoting as large a fraction of its economic output to military purposes as did the Soviet Union during the Cold War, China has steadily expanded its army, navy, and air force, thereby making itself a formidable regional military power. Over time, it is expected to have the forces to operate militarily outside its home region. Specifically, while its ships now patrol its own coastal waters, China is apparently considering building a blue-water navy, complete with aircraft carriers, which would be able to challenge the world's only global navy, that of the United States. The German decision to build a high-seas fleet to confront Britain's then-dominant Royal Navy was, as it happens, one of the developments that led to World War I.

Furthermore, although it is not making obvious preparations to go to war over any of them, China does have border and territorial disputes with several of its neighbors. The map of Asia, including the designation of the boundaries of national territorial waters, is not fully settled. China also has strained relations with Japan. The strains date back to World War II and Japan's brutal occupation of much of the Chinese mainland, an episode with which, in China's eyes more than six decades later, Japan had not fully come to terms, and for which it had not adequately apologized. The communist government in Beijing, it should be noted, has actively sought to keep alive Chinese memories of Japanese atrocities as a way of mobilizing nationalist sentiment on its own behalf.

On one issue, moreover, China has repeatedly declared its readiness to go to war: the status of Taiwan. Although the island has not been governed from Beijing since the communist assumption of power there in 1949 and has functioned as an independent country in virtually every way, the communist regime insists that Taiwan belongs to China and promises to fight in response to a formal declaration of Taiwanese independence. Much of the military force that the Chinese government has built is designed to make good on that promise. The Taiwan Strait separating the island from the mainland qualifies as a particularly dangerous place because hostilities there could draw in the United States, which has an informal commitment to Taiwan's security. In the event of a

Sino-American military clash, two large nuclear-armed powers would be at war with each other.

Taiwan has a particular resonance among Chinese because, having been seized by Japan in 1895 and protected from the mainland by the United States after 1950, it symbolizes the long decades of Chinese submission to the will of foreigners. By all accounts, the commitment to the eventual "reunification" of the island and the mainland pervades every stratum of Chinese society. Taiwan is one issue over which China does seem prepared to challenge the status quo in East Asia by force.

To be sure, the most destabilizing Chinese policies to date have been economic, not military ones. The Chinese government has kept the exchange rate for its currency low by pegging it to the dollar, leading to large annual trade surpluses that it has converted into a large stockpile of dollar reserves. All this has unbalanced the global economy, and the flood of inexpensive Chinese consumer goods to the United States contributed to the crash of September 15, 2008, by helping to keep American prices low, which encouraged the Federal Reserve to keep interest rates low. This in turn made it cheap to borrow money, and much of that cheap money flowed into commercial and residential property, inflating the housing bubble whose bursting worsened the global economic downturn of 2008.

Although they had the effect of disrupting the global economy, none of these Chinese policies was specifically intended to do so; they were intended, rather, to serve Chinese domestic economic and political purposes, in particular to sustain through its low exchange rate the expansion of the country's exporting industries so that Chinese workers could continue to be absorbed into them. The communist authorities apparently deemed this necessary to make their rule acceptable to, if not necessarily popular with, the Chinese people. For Chinese economic policy is premised on the existence of the post-1945 international economic arrangements of which the United States has served as the chief advocate and protector, especially a worldwide openness to the continuing expansion of cross-border trade. China has as great an interest in these arrangements as any other country. Economic considerations make China a champion of the status quo, not a challenger to it.

Economics has the potential to modify Chinese international conduct in other ways: operating a market economy, of the kind that China has developed over three decades, creates the basis for democratic politics; democracies behave, on the whole, in less bellicose fashion than non-democracies. If and as China becomes more democratic, therefore, it will be less likely to adopt policies that threaten its neighbors, at least in military terms. And the multiplying economic ties between China and Taiwan give both parties an additional incentive to avoid armed conflict in the Taiwan Strait.

Taiwan aside, moreover, Chinese military aggression in the service of imperial aggrandizement, a common occurrence in European history before the second half of the twentieth century, is not particularly likely. While throughout its long history China has frequently gone to war, and the country's borders have expanded and contracted over the centuries, Chinese governments have seldom launched military campaigns to extend their control beyond where it now reaches and to subdue peoples who now have independent countries of their own.

Two Chinese military initiatives of the Cold War period underscore this point. China waged a brief war with India in 1962 along the border between the two countries. China's purpose in fighting was to defend its own view of where that border should properly be drawn, which differed from the Indian view, but not to capture what all parties concerned regarded as Indian territory. Although the Chinese forces gained the upper hand in these skirmishes, China did not press its military advantage, as it could have done, to move its forces deeper into India. Similarly, a military incursion into the northern part of Vietnam in 1978 was designed to punish the Vietnamese for policies of which China disapproved, in particular their support for a Cambodian government unfriendly to China. After a short period of occupation, the Chinese withdrew their forces.

Apart from China's imperial traditions, any government in Beijing is bound to be preoccupied, for the foreseeable future, with what will loom as the country's foremost challenge: lifting its huge rural population out of poverty. It is far less likely that the officials who rule China get out of bed each morning eager to assert Chinese power in the world and drive the United States out of East Asia than that their most pressing daily concerns have to do with somehow coping with the rising discontent in inland, rural China, the many protests against one or another of the government's policies that erupt almost daily, and the tens of millions of people who roam the country without permanent employment.

As long as widespread poverty persists—and even with the continuation of double-digit rates of annual economic growth it will persist for decades—the Chinese government's principal focus will be inward. The country's success in combating poverty since the late 1970s has depended, as noted, on the existing international economic institutions and practices, the ones closely identified with the United States. Any effort to overturn the economic and security arrangements in East Asia, let alone globally, will make China poorer, not richer.

Finally, demography works, in the longer run, against a Chinese assault on the world's security and economic orders. China's policy, begun in the Maoist years, of restricting married couples to a single child will produce, by the third decade of the current century, a rapidly aging population. Countries with aging populations are typically not eager for military adventures, if for no other reason than that they lack the surplus youth to fill the ranks of the armed forces.

History does not repeat itself, Mark Twain once said, but it does rhyme. The parallels between early-twentieth-century Germany and early-twenty-first-century China are close enough that concerns that China will follow the German path in challenging the international status quo, which could provoke a confrontation with the United States, are not groundless. But the differences between the two countries and the two eras are substantial enough, and the barriers to disruptive Chinese international conduct robust enough, to make a repetition of the fateful and destructive geopolitics of a hundred years ago anything but certain. China has a number of substantial incentives to accommodate itself to the existing international order that Germany lacked. Indeed, it may be that an end to, rather than the continuation of, China's economic success would turn that country into a threat to peace in East Asia.

The weakening, let alone the end, of the communist regime's proudest achievement, rapid economic growth, would remove one of its two principal sources of political legitimacy, forcing it to rely, in order to remain in power, on the other one: nationalism. An attack on Taiwan without a Taiwanese declaration of independence, if it should occur, is likely to arise from an effort by the government in Beijing to whip up nationalist sentiment to distract the population from hard economic times.

If, for whatever reason, China should come to threaten its neighbors, the United States would have to retrace its strategic footsteps, forsaking the post–Cold War task of reassurance for the more demanding, dangerous, and expensive Cold War mission of deterrence. In that case, the resources available to support deterrence would be less generous than during the Cold War. The United States would also labor under the handicap, in carrying out such a policy, of depending on China to fund a large part of its chronic current account deficit. It is not easy for a country to be on harsh terms with its banker.

If the deterrence of China became necessary, Washington would certainly try to form as broad a coalition as possible. It would seek to include in such a coalition not only its formal Asian allies, Australia, New Zealand, Japan, and South Korea, but also the countries with which it has cultivated informal but increasingly close bilateral and military ties, such as Vietnam and India. With China's growing economic importance, however, and in the absence of the mortal threat that communist China, with its revolutionary Maoist ideology, posed to the rest of Asia, it is unclear how many of them the United States would be able to enlist in the anti-Chinese cause.

"Let China sleep," Napoleon once said. "When she wakes up, the world will be sorry." In the last part of the twentieth century China awakened and the result has been, on balance, good, not bad, for the world. The balance of global gains and losses from this epic event, however, could still shift into the negative column: China could follow a German course, using its growing geopolitical weight to try to refashion the international order in East Asia in ways that threaten the interests of other countries. A revisionist course is not the likeliest direction for China but it is far from impossible.

Either an economically very successful and therefore self-confident Chinese regime or an economically
very unsuccessful and therefore beleaguered one
could well be tempted to assert itself in East Asia in
ways its neighbors find unacceptable, perhaps even
threatening, a temptation that America's reduced fiscal circumstances could enhance. For the Chinese
government's decisions about whether and how to
act on such a temptation would be affected by the resistance it would expect to encounter. That resistance
would depend heavily on American political confidence, the American capacity to attract allies, and the
size and power of the American military forces in the
region. Each of these, in turn, will depend on how
much money the United States has to spend in East
Asia, and in the second decade of the twenty-first
century and beyond, it will have less than in the past.

Still, at the end of the first decade of the twenty-
first century, if the People's Republic of China had not
yet fully become what American officials hoped it
would eventually be—an international stakeholder
committed to upholding existing global economic and
security norms and contributing to their upkeep—
neither did it explicitly oppose, and commit itself to
overturning, these American-supported international
norms. This was something that could not be said
with anything like the same degree of confidence

about the other large, strategically located, and formerly communist potential disturber of the international peace: Russia.

RUSSIA

Russia's importance comes from its size—it is geographically the world's largest country—its substantial stockpile of nuclear weapons, which rivals that of the United States, its considerable reserves of minerals, especially oil and natural gas, and its location. It is part of the world's three most strategically important regions: the Middle East—the Persian Gulf with its even greater energy reserves lies to Russia's southeast; East Asia, via the country's long Pacific coastline and border with China; and Europe, where Russia has functioned as a great power since the time of the tsar Peter the Great in the seventeenth century.

Moreover, Russia was for almost all of its history until the last decade of the twentieth century part of a multinational empire in which Russians ruled other peoples, an empire that for centuries expanded from its Muscovite core eastward and southward until it reached the Black Sea, the Caspian Sea, and the Pacific Ocean. Ultimately it came to span eleven time zones. During the Cold War, Soviet control also extended far into Europe, to the middle of Germany to the west and the Balkans to the south. The drive to conquer territory and the experience of ruling non-Russians against their will is thus normal, not exceptional, in Russian history.

China's historical international greatness is for all twenty-first-century Chinese a distant memory: the country's era of international and even regional primacy had come to an end by the beginning of the nineteenth century. Russia's years of imperial glory as the core of one of the world's two superpowers, by contrast, fall within the living memories of most Russians. In 1991, with the breakup of the Soviet Union, Russia suffered a steep and painful decline in international power and status. Resentment of that decline lingers among many Russians, fueling a wish among some to reverse the course of recent history.

Russia had become, at the end of the first decade of the present century, more overtly committed to altering the global status quo than China. Russian leaders expressed more explicitly than their Chinese counterparts their unhappiness with the international distribution of power and influence. They expressed particular discontent with what they regarded as the undue importance of the United States, occasionally revealing their belief that it was deliberate American policy to weaken and perhaps even dismember Russia. The most powerful Russian leader, Vladimir

Putin, publicly described the fall of the Soviet Union, which left the United States as the sole surviving superpower but also liberated 150 million non-Russians from Russian rule and 150 million Russians from the tyranny of the Communist Party, as the single greatest geopolitical disaster of the twentieth century.

The regime in Moscow came to regard the fourteen non-Russian former republics of the Soviet Union, which all became independent countries in 1991, as an area of special Russian geopolitical prerogatives, calling them, collectively, Russia's "Near Abroad." Russian president Dimitri Medvedev asserted that the region was one of "privileged interest" for his country, suggesting the ambition to exercise some degree of control there.

In August 2008, Russia fought a brief war with Georgia, one of the countries in the Near Abroad, defeating its small army and effectively ratifying the status as Russian protectorates of Abkhazia and South Ossetia, two small pieces of territory legally recognized as part of Georgia. Russian leaders also occasionally proclaimed that they bear special responsibility for the more than 15 million ethnic Russians who live outside the borders of the Russian Federation. Many of these Russians live in neighboring Ukraine, whose independence some in Russia itself find difficult to accept after more than three centuries of Ukrainian inclusion in a larger Russian state. Adolf Hitler's professed concern for Germans living outside Germany, it is perhaps worth noting, provided one of the rationales for the Nazi drive to the east in World War II.

Beyond what was once the Soviet Union, Russia has tried to exert its influence by manipulating its supplies of energy to European countries. Politically motivated interruptions in supply were presumably part of the Russian design to reassert itself globally by becoming an "energy superpower."

Russian leaders may regret the passing of the Soviet Union, but the Soviet Union and the policies it carried out (for which these same leaders also profess nostalgia) produced the Cold War, which divided Europe into two armed camps and sowed conflict throughout the rest of the world. The creeping expansion of NATO toward Russia's borders, and Russia's resistance to it, re-creates one of the Cold War's signal features. All of this suggests that Russia's policies—some of them, to be sure, in part the consequence of American policies—may push the United States to readopt an expensive policy of containment in Europe just as it enters a period of straitened fiscal circumstances. During the Cold War, NATO's Western European allies shared the burden of containing the

Soviet Union. If a new policy of containment were to become necessary, the Europeans, encumbered with large welfare states and slow growth rates, dependent on Russian natural gas and, partly for that reason, ambivalent about the dangers Russia poses, might well be reluctant to contribute to it.

As with China there are reasons to doubt that Russia will mount a stiff challenge to the American-led security order in Europe, although they are not all the same reasons as those that will likely restrain China. The principal difference between the two countries is that while China is a rising power, Russia is a declining one. China is destined to become stronger as the twenty-first century unfolds: Russia is likely to grow weaker.

The collapse of the Soviet Union left a Russian successor state with half the Soviet population, whose major demographic trend works against its aspirations for great international influence. The country is shrinking. It has a high mortality rate and thus an unusually low life expectancy—less than sixty years for males—due to epidemics of cardiovascular disease and alcoholism and to widespread tuberculosis and HIV/AIDS. Like all European countries, Russia has a low birthrate. Its population is therefore decreasing, by 700,000 people each year. Russia is on course to lose 20 million people between 1990 and 2025 and by 2050 may have a population of only 100 million rather than the 150 million it had at the dawn of the post-Soviet era in 1991.

Nor are its economic prospects much brighter. Its national income soared in the first decade of the twenty-first century because of a rapid rise in the price of energy, of which it is a major exporter. The authoritarian regime of Vladimir Putin did nothing during these boom years, however, to cultivate other sources of economic growth, making Russia's economic fortunes hostage to the price of fossil fuels.

Nor did the Putin regime, despite its sometimes bellicose rhetoric, take the opportunity that its energy windfall presented to rebuild to any significant extent the armed forces that had collapsed, along with the other institutions that had served the Soviet Union, after 1991. A country with, in effect, a one-crop economy, a shrinking population, and modest non-nuclear military forces is not a strong candidate to wield great power in the international system.

Nor, even if the country were (or were likely to become) stronger than it is, would it be easy for Russia to resume its long career as an imperial state. In the two decades following the end of the Soviet Union the territories that once were imperial possessions solidified their common status as independent countries, with working institutions—imperfect ones, to be sure, in most cases—and distinct national identities.

Finally, although the Russian economy has, aside from energy, performed less well than the Chinese one, like the Chinese economy it has the potential to restrain aggressive foreign policies in two ways. First, like China, Russia depends on the American-centered open international economic order. Without access to well-functioning global markets the country's major source of revenue—energy—would lose much of its value. Second, in Russia, as in China and as in every country, the working of a market economy tends, over the long term, to create the basis for political democracy, and democracies tend to carry out more cooperative, less aggressive policies toward their neighbors than do authoritarian governments of the kind that Russia had in 2010.

A Russian challenge to regional security arrangements that exerts pressure on the United States to make costly and therefore politically difficult increases in its contribution to European security is not, therefore, the most probable course for Russian foreign policy in the second decade of the twenty-first century and beyond. But such a challenge is far from impossible, and, like a comparable Chinese challenge in East Asia, it would require an American shift from a policy of reassurance back to one of deterrence. If a challenge should occur, it is more likely to arise out of Russian weakness than Russian strength. As in China, the political legitimacy that Russia's undemocratic regime enjoys rests on two pillars: economic success and an ostentatious commitment to defend the nation's interests against allegedly predatory foreigners.

To the extent that the economy falters and Putin or his successors come to rely on showy displays of nationalism, they are more likely to initiate quarrels with their neighbors. Russian weakness will make the kind of leaders it had in the first decade of the new century more inclined to contest the existing world order. As with its Chinese counterpart, whether and how the Russian government acts on such inclinations will depend on the resistance it anticipates meeting, which will in turn depend greatly on how much resistance the United States is able to muster.

In theory, the United States and its European allies have already made provision for such a contingency by expanding their alliance, NATO, eastward. In fact, NATO offers at best a weak and uncertain hedge against Russian revisionism in Europe. For one thing, membership has conspicuously not been offered to the most likely victims of Russian predation, Ukraine and Georgia. The alliance has declined to include them, contrary to American declarations that no country (except Russia itself) would be excluded, precisely because Russia's strenuous objections made it clear that a commitment to defend these particular countries might actually have to be honored one day. Furthermore, as NATO expansion proceeded, the American Congress and the American public were reassured by the Clinton and George W. Bush administrations that the addition of new members would require no additional American military deployments, no further resources for European security, and no sacrifice of any kind from Americans. These political circumstances combine with the impending economic constraints on public policies of all kinds to make the United States less than ideally positioned to discourage and, if it should occur, to hold in check a Russian challenge to twenty-first-century European security arrangements. NATO expansion has given the United States the worst of both worlds: it has made dangerous Russian behavior more likely while rendering America less capable of responding effectively to such behavior.

To summarize: China and Russia are the two countries in a position to turn the economic constraints that will bind the United States into a setback and, in the worst case, a disaster for international security. A challenge to regional security arrangements by either or both is not inconceivable: each has grievances against the status quo in its own neighborhood and globally. Because the United States acts as the chief supporter of the status quo in East Asia, Europe, and the world at large, and because American foreign policy will have to operate under stricter limits than at any time in the past seven decades, such a challenge would come at a particularly inopportune moment in world history. The forces discouraging such a challenge do seem on balance to be stronger than the ones pushing China and Russia toward policies that would provoke a confrontation with the United States. The twenty-first century seems tilted toward peace, but this tilt is scarcely irreversible, and if it should be reversed, America's fiscal position will hamper efforts to cope with the reversal.

To put it another way, as long as the world's security and economic orders depend ultimately on the United States to sustain them, and the active exercise of American power is limited by economic considerations, global security and prosperity may be said to rest on something of a bluff. China and Russia are the countries in a position to call that bluff. The odds are—insofar as it is possible to calculate odds on the unknowable geopolitical future and the direction of the internal politics of two large, complicated countries with secretive governments—that neither will do so; but this is merely probable, not certain.

Even in that best case, however, even without the revival of the classic, age-old cut and thrust of ambition and fear backed by military force among the great powers of the international system, the danger of aggressive foreign policies with potentially far-reaching, damaging consequences will not have disappeared from the face of the earth. That danger will still be present in yet another part of the world where the United States has come to play an important, and expensive, military and political role: the Middle East.

CHAPTER FIVE

THE HEART OF GEOPOLITICS

THE MIDDLE EAST

During the Cold War, of all the world's regions Europe and East Asia mattered most for American security policy. It was there that the United States deployed the majority of its armed forces. The war they were prepared to wage in Europe fortunately never took place, but America did become engaged in two serious conflicts in East Asia. By the first decade of the twenty-first century the focus of global security and American security policy had shifted to the Middle East. This region, consisting of the Arab world and the territory surrounding the Persian Gulf including Iran, had become the main theater of American military operations. As such, it was the focus of what are normally the most economically expensive and politically controversial foreign policies that a country undertakes. The major test of the American capacity to sustain the main elements of its global role in an era of economic scarcity will come in the Middle East.

The shift of American focus took place because the three great ideas whose spread brought historically unprecedented tranquillity to Europe and to a lesser extent to East Asia—peace, democracy, and free markets—did not take hold in the Middle East. For most of the countries in the region, war is neither unthinkable, as in Europe, nor unlikely, as in East Asia. To the contrary, almost all are involved, to one degree or another, in geopolitical competition, contested borders, expensive arms races, and occasionally war itself. From the Middle East, moreover, have come much of the ideological inspiration and the financing for twenty-first-century terrorism, as well as many of the terrorists themselves.

Not coincidentally, none of the governments in the region except Turkey and Israel has ever had a democratic government or a fully developed market economy: governments' roles in economic affairs in the Middle East are more extensive than in the West.

Peace, democracy, and free markets do not dominate the politics, economics, and international relations of Africa, either, and that continent has served as a breeding ground for terrorism as well; but Africa attracts far less attention from the United States because it lacks, among other things, a particular kind of threat to American interests that is found in the Middle East: the one posed by nuclear weapons.

Nuclear weapons preoccupied the United States during the Cold War but American officials were then concerned with the large stockpile controlled by the Soviet Union. With the end of the Cold War, what had been a secondary although serious issue came to the fore: nuclear proliferation—the spread of nuclear weapons to countries (and even rogue groups) not previously in possession of them. The Middle East is a region ripe for proliferation; Africa is not. Nuclear proliferation seems particularly menacing to the United States, to its friends and allies, and to global order in general, for two reasons.

First, the more independent centers of control of nuclear weapons there are, the more likely it seems that one of them will eventually order a nuclear attack, with all the horrific destruction that it will cause: proliferation makes nuclear war more likely. Second, nuclear weapons make their owners more powerful, so nuclear proliferation can turn a government unfriendly to American and Western interests from a nuisance into a serious danger. It can shift the balance of power in the region such as the Middle East in a threatening direction.

Nuclear proliferation actually occurred in South Asia two years before the new century began, when India and Pakistan both exploded nuclear devices, and a nuclear-armed Pakistan, with its unstable government and terrorism-sponsoring Islamic fundamentalist groups, had become by the end of the twenty-first century's first decade a major problem for the United States and the world. South Asia becomes all the more problematic if it is defined to include Afghanistan, the base from which al Qaeda attacked the United States on September 11, 2001, and where American troops subsequently waged an ongoing battle against a nasty insurgency. Yet Afghanistan and Pakistan, dangerous though they are, lack what in the end makes the Middle East so important for American interests and global security: oil.

Because it is the fuel for approximately 90 percent of the planet's transportation, it is almost literally the case that the world runs on oil. Certainly no industrial economy or urban society could currently function without it. Almost two-thirds of the world's readily accessible reserves of oil are located in countries with borders on the Persian Gulf. It is the region's colossal endowment of the most valuable mineral on Earth that has drawn the United States to the Middle East.

The American government's strategic interest in the modern Middle East dates from 1945, when President Franklin D. Roosevelt, on his way home from the World War II summit meeting with British Prime Minister Winston Churchill and Soviet leader Joseph Stalin at the Black Sea port of Yalta, met King Abdul Aziz of Saudi Arabia on an American destroyer docked at the entrance to the Suez Canal. The Saudi kingdom, radically different from the United States in every significant way, had attracted the attention of the United States because of the enormous deposits of oil beneath its sands, which Western oil companies had begun to exploit. During the Cold War, the United States developed another interest in the Middle East, as it did in every other part of the world: minimizing the influence of its great political and military rival, the Soviet Union.

As exports from Saudi Arabia and its neighbors came to account for an ever larger part of the world's total consumption of petroleum, the United States took on an oil-related task: patrolling the seas and oceans through which Persian Gulf oil had to pass to reach the countries that increasingly depended on it for powering their farms and factories and running their cars, trucks, buses, and airplanes. Japan, for example, had to import more than 90 percent of its oil from the region. It became one of the missions of the U.S. Navy to protect, and therefore to guarantee, the world's supply of oil.

Beginning in the 1950s American security policy periodically faced yet another kind of challenge in the Middle East: the rise of radically inclined regimes that attempted to dominate the region, threatening to tilt the local balance of power against the United States and its oil-producing friends and, in the worst case, to take control of the region's oil fields. Egypt under Gamal Abdel Nasser emerged as the first such challenger when it seized control of the Suez Canal in 1956. Nasser's political standing collapsed with Israel's sweeping military victory over his country, as well as Syria and Jordan, in June 1967. In 1979 a revolution in Iran toppled the hereditary ruler, the Shah, and brought to power anti-Western clerics dedicated to spreading their fundamentalist Islamic message and exerting Iranian influence throughout the region and in Muslim countries beyond it. A third regional challenge came from Iraq's dictator, Saddam Hussein, who consolidated supreme power in the same year as the Iranian Revolution, against which he launched a war that lasted for more than eight years. In the aftermath of that war, for much of the 1990s, the United States opposed both Iran and Iraq, pursuing a strategy of "dual containment" toward them. The American armed forces fought two wars against Saddam's army, in 1991 and 2003, with the second destroying his regime and leading to a protracted and difficult American occupation.

In its decades-long effort to prevent the domination of the Middle East and its oil supplies by a hostile power, the United States conformed to the nineteenth-century British statesman Lord Palmerston's dictum that his country had no permanent friends and no permanent adversaries, only permanent interests. At different times the American government found itself both opposed to and allied with all three aspirants to regional hegemony. After 1973 Egypt, once America's Middle Eastern nemesis, joined the American camp; Iran under the Shah was an American ally, under the mullahs a bitter enemy; and during the Iraq-Iran war the American government provided modest assistance to the same Saddam Hussein against whom it subsequently waged two wars.

Through all the twists and turns of American policy in the region, however, a single interest—ensuring the unimpeded flow of oil—remained constant. Oil also served as the midwife of the most conspicuous

and longest-running American initiative in the region: its effort to broker a settlement between Israel
and its Arab neighbors. Because it had the strongest
local military forces, and because it invariably attracted the enmity of the radical powers of the Middle East, Israel consistently served as a strategic asset
to the United States, helping to check the regimes
that threatened American interests; cultural and political affinities bound the two countries together as
well. Israel was also at odds, however, with America's
Arab clients.

In response to American military assistance to Israel in its 1973 war against Egypt and Syria, the ordinarily pro-American Arab oil producers attempted
to impose an embargo on oil shipments to the United
States, as well as to the Netherlands. Oil being a
globally traded commodity, they could not success-
fully single out these two countries, but the reductions they made in their exports did cause the global
price of oil to soar. To persuade the Arabs to increase
production and relieve the upward pressure on the
oil price, American Secretary of State Henry
Kissinger undertook energetic mediation between Israel and its adversaries.

Although no further embargoes were attempted,
the United States continued its efforts to settle the
Arab-Israeli conflict for the next thirty-five years. It

achieved some significant successes, in the form of Israeli-Egyptian and Israeli-Jordanian peace treaties. The American diplomatic efforts continued through seven presidential administrations. Indeed, they came to be expected of any American chief executive: success brought approval at home and abroad, failure seemingly had little or no cost, and most Israelis and American friends of Israel supported these efforts most of the time.

American mediation continued, as well, because the leaders of the Arab countries aligned with the United States insisted that the unresolved conflict with Israel was the largest obstacle to peace throughout the region and presented the greatest single threat to their political survival and to American interests in the Middle East. Although they often said this, however, there was little evidence that they believed it, and one reason that they did not believe it was that it was not true. The Arab-Israeli conflict was only one of many in the Middle East, and resolving it would do nothing to end the disputes between, for example, Sunni and Shia Muslims, or Arab nationalists and Islamic fundamentalists. Moreover, Israel and its policies did not pose a serious threat to the Arab regimes or to American interests in the Middle East. The serious danger to both came from the Islamic Republic of Iran.

The twenty-first-century challenge that Iran presents resembles the issue around which American foreign policy was organized for most of the second half of the twentieth century: the Soviet threat to Europe. Western Europe then, like the Middle East now, was a crucial region for the United States, one where the local governments could not be counted on to defend themselves: in Europe because when the United States first assumed responsibility for its defense European societies had been shattered by World War II; in the Middle East because the Arab regimes are weak, lack popular legitimacy, and for the most part have ineffective military forces.

Iran now, like the Soviet Union then, is larger than any of the countries it threatens and has a long history of conflict with them: the animosity between Persians and Arabs dates back centuries. Like the Soviet Union, the Islamic Republic of Iran is a state created out of a violent revolution and based on a radical ideology that puts it in opposition to its neighbors, an ideology that it attempts to spread through any tactics that offer promise of success including the use of force. Just as the Soviet Union sought to subvert the non-communist governments to its west through local communist parties, for example, so Iran has tried to make use of its fellow Shia Muslims living in majority Sunni countries to expand its influence.

The Soviet Union of the Cold War and Iran of the post–Cold War era differ in one major way: the magnitude of their power. The Soviet Union was a multinational empire of 300 million people and geographically the largest country on the planet, with an enormous military establishment that had defeated Germany's mighty Wehrmacht in four bitter years of fighting in World War II. It deployed tens of thousands of nuclear weapons, and its land, sea, and air forces were capable of operating all over the world. The Islamic Republic of Iran, by contrast, is a medium-sized country of 72 million people with very modest military forces that struggled to battle those of its smaller neighbor, Iraq, to a standoff in the 1980s. Iran's armed forces have no capacity to conduct operations beyond the Middle East. This difference has made it cheaper and easier for the United States to deal with Iran in the twenty-first century than it was to cope with the Soviet Union during the Cold War, but the American strategic mission was the same in both cases: deterrence.

During the Cold War, the American armed forces were organized and deployed so as to dissuade the Soviet Union from launching a military campaign to seize Western Europe. The task was made both more urgent and more dangerous by the fact that both countries had nuclear weapons. Twenty-first-century

Iran aspires to have them as well. Should it obtain them, the United States would have a new incentive to provide protection for the other countries of the Middle East: nuclear weapons can only be reliably offset by other nuclear weapons, and while the United States already has them, Iran's neighbors do not and would have to acquire them to ensure their own security. Absent an American guarantee, therefore, the need to deter Iran would likely generate a burst of nuclear proliferation. To be sure, Israel is widely believed to have nuclear weapons and so would be able to practice nuclear deterrence against Iran. But Israeli nuclear weapons would not protect the Arab countries. Saudi Arabia might be willing to rely for its protection against Iran on American, but not on Israeli, nuclear deterrence. Deterring a nuclear-armed Iran would not necessarily be appreciably more expensive than keeping in check a non-nuclear Iran, but it might well be politically more complex. It would reprise the Cold War American policy of providing nuclear deterrence against the Soviet Union for Western Europe because it would involve a promise to defend, with nuclear weapons if necessary, countries within range of an Iranian attack but separated from the continental United States by thousands of miles. To ensure that the Soviet Union

believed that the United States would defend Western Europe—to make the policy of deterrence credible in the eyes of the Soviet leaders—American
policy-makers deemed it necessary to station American forces on the European continent. The American troops were, on the whole, welcome there and
their presence caused relatively little friction between America and Europe. If the American government decided that the credible deterrence of a
nuclear-armed Iran required the presence of American forces in the Arab countries being defended,
however, these troops would not, for cultural and political reasons, receive a similarly cordial reception.
To the contrary, such a policy would create political
difficulties both for the host governments and for the
United States.

Even if the deterrence of a nuclear-armed Iran
should turn out to be both inexpensive and relatively
free of political friction, it would have an inherent
drawback: it would require an open-ended effort. Iran
would remain a serious threat even with extensive
American diplomatic engagement with the Islamic
Republic. There was, after all, considerable Soviet-
American engagement during the Cold War, in the
form of regular diplomatic contact, cultural ex-
changes, athletic contests, summit meetings, and

elaborate negotiations concerning arms limitations. None of these relieved the United States of the need to maintain a robust policy of deterrence in Europe and around the world. Deterrence is a policy akin to managing a chronic, incurable disease. Braced by the magnitude of the Soviet threat and mindful of the disastrous consequences of failing to stand up to totalitarian powers in the 1930s, the American public supported the policy of deterring the Soviet regime for four decades. Americans might not, however, be so steadfast toward the less formidable Iran in the economically straitened circumstances of the second decade of the twenty-first century and beyond, especially because personal memories of Hitler and World War II (and even the Cold War itself) are growing dimmer.

The collapse of the Soviet Union and its fragmentation into fifteen separate sovereign states paved the way for the emergence of a new, less ideological, less aggressive Russia, which did not pose the same threat to its neighbors. It did not dominate Central and Eastern Europe and so no longer threatened the countries of Western Europe. For geopolitical as well as for ideological reasons, therefore, post-Soviet Russia did not have to be deterred as the Soviet Union had had to be. Partly inspired by what happened in

Europe in 1989 and 1991, during the first two post–Cold War decades the United States attempted to bring about a similar transformation in the Middle East. The American government carried out two sets of policies, each intended to transform the region and thus dramatically ease the burden of defending Western and global interests there. They failed, but a third transformative strategy does have the potential to make that burden lighter.

The Clinton administration devoted a great deal of time and effort to trying to broker final political settlements between Israel and two of its neighbors: Syria to the north, and the Palestine Liberation Organization (PLO), the representative of the Palestinians living to Israel's east between the pre-1967 armistice line and the Jordan River as well as in the Gaza Strip to Israel's south. Arab-Israeli peacemaking became the highest priority of the foreign policy of this administration, which believed that an overall settlement would make it much easier to assure American interests in the Middle East. These, of course, included the uninterrupted outflow of its oil.

The Clinton administration did not succeed in producing the agreements that it sought. Although the Israeli government offered territorial concessions of the magnitude that had been almost universally assumed to be adequate to satisfy the demands of its neighbors, in the end both Hafez al-Asad, the dictator of Syria, and Yasir Arafat, the autocratic leader of the PLO, refused these offers, preferring instead to continue their respective conflicts with Israel. Lacking the political legitimacy that democracy confers, and having failed to deliver any economic improvements to the people they governed, both men had come to rely on the conflict with Israel, and their own adamant commitment to prosecuting it, for such popular support as they enjoyed. For them, and for other Arab leaders as well, the Arab-Israeli conflict was too valuable an asset to give up. Nor can an explanation for the persistence of this particular Middle Eastern conflict omit the genuinely and deeply held belief in the Arab world that Jews, being neither Arab nor Muslim, are not entitled to their own sovereign state in the region.

Nor, even if a territorial and political settlement between Israel and all its neighbors could be achieved, would this end, or even substantially attenuate, the many other Middle Eastern conflicts, some of which are far older and bloodier than the one between Arabs and Israelis. As a way to make American policy in the region cheaper and easier, therefore, what came to be known as the "peace process" failed and, even if the specific negotiations that it involved had come to fruition, was never likely to make the Middle East entirely safe for American interests.

The administration of George W. Bush, who succeeded Bill Clinton as the American president, adopted a different approach to the transformation of the Middle East: the promotion of democracy in the region. This approach came about partly by accident. For reasons having nothing to do with democracy, the United States attacked Iraq, deposed Saddam Hussein as its ruler, and then found itself, contrary to the administration's wishes and expectations, occupying the country and facing the task of establishing a new government there. It was natural for the United States, given its deep and abiding commitment to democratic principles, to seek to make the government it established a democratic one. Having made a commitment to democracy in Iraq, the president broadened that commitment to include the entire region, with the promise, or at least the hope, that the advent of democracy throughout the Middle East would transform the region in a way that would make it more congenial to, and less burdensome for, the United States.

Iraq held a series of more or less free and fair elections, as did Lebanon. The Egyptian government, however, which maintained close ties to and received generous annual aid payments from the United States, staged a presidential election that was neither free nor fair, and elections that seemed to meet both standards in the Palestinian territories were won by Hamas, an Islamic fundamentalist group that openly sponsored terrorism and was committed to an anti-Western program that included the destruction of the state of Israel. Elsewhere in the Arab world, despite the Bush administration's urging, the ruling autocrats, even those most dependent on the United States, showed no sign of permitting democracy to take root.

Success in promoting democracy throughout the Middle East would surely change the region in ways favorable to American interests. This would be the case, however, only if the countries there were to become genuine democracies, incorporating into their political systems not only the selection of the government by popular vote but also the defense of liberty—the protection of economic, religious, and political freedom. Because genuine democracies tend to conduct more cooperative, less militant foreign policies than non-democracies, if the Bush project for the Middle East were actually to succeed, the international relations of the region would come to resemble those of twenty-first-century Europe, which would

make the safeguarding of American and global interests there far easier.

Ironically, the Middle Eastern country best prepared for democracy turned out to be the one most
threatening to the United States. The Iranian regime
staged a presidential election in 2009 in which only
its officially approved candidates could run. When
the election was apparently stolen from one of these
candidates on behalf of another—the incumbent,
Mahmoud Ahmadinejad—millions of people took to
the streets to protest. The spontaneous public partic-
ipation in the demonstrations throughout the country
suggested that the Iranian people both want and are
capable of operating a democratic political system. In
that case, the obstacle to Iranian democracy—and
therefore, perhaps, to a far less aggressive, ideologi-
cally motivated foreign policy—is the commitment
of the theocratic regime to use force to remain in
power.

Arab governments were also willing to turn their
guns on the people they governed to keep themselves
in power, but in the Arab countries the demand for
free elections and especially for the freedoms of
speech, the press, and religion seemed considerably
weaker than among their Persian neighbors. The absence of the relevant values, skills, and traditions, as
well as the vigilant opposition to it of the armed

forces and secret police forces the regimes controlled, obstructed the spread of democracy in the Arab world.

Neither the Arab-Israeli peace process nor the promotion of democracy therefore seems a promising way to lighten the burden of American foreign policy, in an era of reduced resources, in the one part of the world where the effort required of the United States will certainly remain substantial. There is, however, a third means to this end, one that would gradually alter the region so as to diminish the threat to American and global interests. Unlike the other two strategies, this approach to the transformation of the Middle East and its role in global security affairs lies within the power of the United States to implement. This third mechanism for transformation is to reduce the American consumption of oil.

Oil

Because the United States accounts for so much of the world's oil usage, a major reduction in American consumption could lower overall consumption enough to reduce the global price of the commodity. This would decrease the money accruing to the governments that depend heavily, in some cases almost exclusively, on the sale of oil to finance their operations. Iran is one such country. The sale of oil accounts for 80 percent of its annual revenue. Reducing the income of the Islamic Republic would give its rulers less money to spend on the policies that threaten the rest of the region and the world, including its ongoing effort to acquire nuclear weapons and a fleet of missiles to deliver them to distant targets and its shipments of funds and weapons to two terrorist organizations, Hamas in the Gaza Strip and Hezbollah in Lebanon.

Restricting the stream of Iranian oil revenue would have an even more powerful effect on the regime: it would undermine its internal stability. The Islamic Republic depends, for its survival, on the support of constituencies that themselves rely on money from the state treasury: the militia known as the Revolutionary Guards, for instance, and employees of the country's large government-funded commercial monopolies. The Iranian government buys such loyalty as it enjoys within the country. Fewer resources would result in less loyalty.

In seeking to stop the mullahs' nuclear weapon program the American government has tried, without success, to persuade other countries to join the United States in imposing economic sanctions on

Iran. A sharp reduction in oil revenues, for which a sharp reduction in American oil consumption is a necessary condition, would have precisely the impact that Washington has vainly sought to produce through international agreement.

A cutback in the American consumption of oil, leading to a reduction in the income oil generates for the countries that export it, would make the Middle East less troublesome for the United States and the world in ways that go beyond the impact on Iran. Notably, it would reduce the resources at the disposal of the government and political elite of Saudi Arabia. While nominally, and in some ways actually, an ally of the United States, Saudi Arabia has also contributed to the difficulties the United States has encountered in the Middle East through the propagation of its official ideology, an extreme form of Islamic fundamentalism known as Wahhabism.

This ideology inspired many of the Middle Eastern terrorists who have attacked Western targets, including the perpetrators of the attacks on New York and Washington of September 11, 2001. In the three airplanes that were hijacked to mount these attacks, eighteen of the twenty-one hijackers were Saudi nationals. The Saudi government pays for many of the madrassas—the religious schools—in Pakistan and

Afghanistan as well as in its own country, in which students who later join extremist groups receive fundamentalist indoctrination. Some of the money that flows from gasoline-buying Americans to the Saudi treasury finds its way, often via wealthy Saudi sympathizers, into the coffers of these same extremist groups, including al Qaeda. Thus it is that the United States is waging a war against terrorism and funding both sides. Using less oil would reduce the money going to the side that Americans do *not* wish to support.

If the United States consumed less oil this would bring yet another benefit to its Middle Eastern policies. The less the world relies on oil, and therefore the less it relies on oil from that region, the less important to the rest of the world the region will be. True, the United States gets relatively little of the oil it imports directly from the Persian Gulf. Since oil is a fungible, globally traded commodity, however, any disturbance in its outflow from the Gulf would automatically, and negatively, affect the United States, in the first instance by increasing the price that Americans, along with everyone else, would have to pay for gasoline. Even if, as is not the case, the flow of oil from the Gulf affected only those countries directly consuming it—Japan above all—the global scope of

American interests and commitments means that the United States would be harmed by any interruption in its supply from the region. Reducing the importance of that supply, no matter who consumes it, would therefore lower the stakes and lighten the burden of American engagement in the Middle East.

To be sure, the world will not be able to do entirely without oil from the Persian Gulf for many decades. The global transportation fleet will need petroleum to operate far into the twenty-first century, and perhaps beyond. But substantially reducing the planet's use of oil would shift the balance of power between producers and consumers in favor of consumers— that is, in favor of the United States, its friends, its allies, and all the countries with large industrial economies. Indeed, given the expected growth in demand for oil in Asia, especially in China and India, a reduction in consumption by the United States will be necessary to prevent overall oil consumption from a steep rise that would tilt the balance further toward the producers and make the Middle East even more important than it is now for the rest of the world. The anticipated growth in global demand in the second and third decades of this century places the world, where oil is concerned, metaphorically on a treadmill moving in the wrong direction. The consuming countries will have to take significant measures to suppress consumption simply to avoid worsening the adverse global trends that oil fosters.

Substantially reducing the consumption of oil in the United States would have, from the American point of view, a positive effect on the policies of troublesome countries even beyond the Middle East, countries whose governments, like those of Iran and Saudi Arabia, depend on oil revenues. Venezuela is one of them. In the first decade of the new century Hugo Chavez, its leader, made himself Latin America's major opponent of the United States. He used the revenues from the country's exports of oil to buy popularity among sectors of Venezuelan society, bestow favors on communist Cuba, and promote himself around the world as a figure of significance. Without these revenues he would hardly have attracted notice beyond his country's borders and probably could not have survived in power, or perhaps even achieved high office in the first place.

Russia is another country whose twenty-first-century foreign policy runs on oil money. It was not the reflexively anti-American policies that its leader, Vladimir Putin, carried out, or his steady suppression of domestic political opposition, that earned him the impressively high approval ratings he received from his countrymen through this century's first decade. He owed his popularity, rather, to the windfall oil profits that accrued to Russia, which the government used to pay pensions and salaries to a grateful public. Without oil revenues Putin, like Chavez, would not have had the resources to carry out policies antagonistic to the United States and might not have been able to remain president (and then prime minister) of his country.

The sharp fall in the price of oil occasioned by the global recession following the events of September 15, 2008, put a dent in the popularity of the Putin regime, offering a preview of its likely fate if Russia's oil revenues should go into permanent decline. In fact, the decrease in the global oil price in the 1980s played a role in the demise of the Soviet Union itself. The loss in income made more urgent the economic reforms undertaken by the last Soviet leader, Mikhail Gorbachev, which set in motion the events that culminated in the Soviet collapse.

Reducing American oil consumption would even help to ease a potential source of friction with China. That country is a net importer rather than an exporter of oil. Its dependence on oil will rise steadily as its economy expands. That dependence is a possible source of international discord. The diplomacy of the Chinese government since the beginning of the new century has sought to ensure reliable supplies of the raw materials the country's industries require, most of which are not found within its borders. This has led to friendly relations with odious regimes governing resource-rich countries, such as the one in Sudan even as it was waging a murderous war against the people of Darfur.

China's drive to secure resources, especially oil, could bring it into military conflict with the United States. The most likely incentive for China to build a major naval force that could challenge the U.S. Navy would be a decision by the Chinese government that the country's security required a Chinese force to safeguard the sea lanes through which oil reaches the Chinese mainland. The less important oil becomes, and the less pressure there is to ensure the supply of it, the weaker that incentive will be.

Substantially reducing the role of oil in the American, Chinese, and global economies would, over the long term, lower the cost of America's international obligations in one final way: it would enhance the prospects for democracy, and therefore for democratically inspired peaceful foreign policies. Oil is the enemy of democracy. Countries that depend on large reserves of it for most of their income almost never have democratic governments. For this there are two main reasons.

First, with the money that flows to the government from the sale of oil comes the temptation for those in charge of the government to do whatever is necessary to maintain power and thus access to that money, rather than submitting themselves to the will of the public through democratic elections. Second, oil-rich countries tend not to develop the institutions of a free-market economy: they don't need them to achieve prosperity. But it is precisely the experience of operating these institutions—private property, a working financial system, a proper legal order—that over time promotes democratic politics. Deprived of their very large oil revenues, Iran and Russia, for example, would have to earn their way in the world by establishing effective free-market economies. If they were able to do so, they would set in motion internal forces that promote democratic governance. Democracy would, on the whole and all other things being equal, incline them to less hostile, more cooperative foreign policies.

Appreciably reducing the role of oil in the global economy and in the politics and economics of the oil-exporting countries would, in sum, have broad and favorable consequences for international security, and especially for the tasks that have fallen to the United States to carry out. So substantial and so favorable would such consequences be that the reduction of its use of oil qualifies as the single most important thing the United States could do to achieve its international goals. As such, cutting back on oil consumption bears comparison with the central strategic mission of the United States for most of the second half of the twentieth century: containment.

The New Containment

During the Cold War the United States adopted as its chief foreign policy goal preventing the international communist movement, led by the Soviet Union, from spreading its influence and its direct control to non-communist parts of the world. The original policy of containment sought to protect Western Europe but was subsequently broadened to include much of the rest of the world.

At the outset the policy relied on political and economic tools. The American program of economic assistance to Western Europe, the Marshall Plan, which was launched in 1947, aimed to foster economic recovery from the shattering effects of war in the recipient countries in order to make them invulnerable to the political appeal of communism and to communist subversion. After the outbreak of the Korean War in 1950, containment became mainly a military effort. The United States deployed a large army in West Germany to block a Soviet attack on Western Europe, maintained a large stockpile of nuclear weapons to offset the comparable Soviet arsenal, acquired military bases in and provided military assistance to many countries around the world, and waged two substantial wars, in Korea and Indochina—all for the purpose of resisting the spread of communism. With this Cold War policy of containment, a reduction in American oil consumption has three important features in common.

First, like containment, it is central to American purposes in the world. Just as almost every policy the United States carried out beyond its borders from the mid-1940s to the beginning of the 1990s was connected in some way to the task of resisting communist power and influence, so reducing American dependence on oil would help to alleviate most of the major problems of international security the United States faces.

Second, containment was a protracted policy, lasting for decades, and for most of that period had a defensive purpose. Far from hoping to overthrow its adversary, for most of the Cold War the United States thought of itself as struggling to hold the line against a powerful foe, to keep communism in check and to prevent the American position in the world from deteriorating. Similarly, it will not be possible for the United States and the other democracies to wean themselves from imported oil quickly or easily. Reducing oil consumption, like containment, will have to be a protracted effort, one whose success may well be judged, at least at first, by whether it prevents a sharp increase in American and global dependence on Middle Eastern petroleum. Like containment, it will have to span multiple presidential administrations and have the unwavering support of both political parties.

Third, the policy of containment generally succeeded in preventing major setbacks for the United States and its allies and ultimately helped to create the conditions in which communism in Europe collapsed because the American public was willing to pay for it with its tax dollars over several decades. While it did not involve the degree of national mobilization or the level of sacrifice that waging and winning World War II had required of the United States, containment was not free. Over its lifetime, Americans annually devoted between 5 and 10 percent of their total national income to defense spending, virtually all of which supported the containment, in one way or another, of communism.

Cutting back on the consumption of petroleum also has a cost, and here America's most important post–Cold War foreign policy project differs from the containment of the Cold War era. Sustaining the earlier policy by maintaining a political consensus in favor of paying for it posed a challenge to the United States. For more than four decades the American public proved equal to that challenge. Paying the price necessary for the gradual reduction of the country's reliance on oil, with all the global benefits that would follow, presents a similar test, but in the first decade of the twenty-first century this was a test that the United States failed miserably.

The way to reduce oil consumption is simple and well known: raise the price of gasoline. A higher price would have two complementary effects. It would lead to conservation. People would use less gasoline. In the short term they would drive their cars less and make more frequent use of public transportation. Over the long term they would demand fuel-efficient vehicles, which carmakers would then have an economic incentive to produce. At the same time, a higher gasoline price would encourage substitution:

fuels other than oil would become economically viable. Entrepreneurs would have a major incentive to invest in the large-scale production of liquid fuels made from plants, for example. With a high enough gasoline price, cars that dispense with liquid fuel altogether and draw their power from battery-generated electricity would become economically attractive.

A crucial feature that conservation and substitution have in common is innovation, which is the process by which relevant new technologies are created. The gradual, incremental improvement of existing products is just as important a form of innovation as is the invention of entirely new ones, and both require investment. The greater the investment in them, the more rapidly innovations of both kinds that promote the more efficient use of oil and the wider use of oil substitutes will appear. Investment, in turn, requires a price signal. Oil is the cheapest and most efficient fuel for transportation; that is why it became the dominant source of power for the world's air and surface fleets. Large sums of money will not be invested in methods for conserving oil and in substitutes for it without the assurance that the price of gasoline will be high enough that it will be economically rewarding to use less of it and that the alternative fuels can compete with it on price.

When the price of internationally traded oil, and therefore gasoline, soared as a result of the two oil shocks of the 1970s, consumers in the United States and elsewhere did cut back on their use of gasoline and money did flow into substitutes for it. To put the United States firmly on the path away from ever-greater dependence on oil, however, will require action by the American government. A government-imposed increase in the price of gasoline in the United States, either through a substantial tax on gasoline at the pump or a price below which the cost of imported oil will not be permitted to fall, or both, is needed, for two reasons.

First, this would assure potential investors in new fuels and fuel-efficient vehicles that the price of oil will remain high, rather than, as occurred after the two oil shocks, falling back to levels at which innovations in alternatives to it cease to be profitable. Second, a high price for American consumers is particularly important because not only does the United States consume more oil than any other country, but it is also the country from which, with the price of oil appropriately and permanently high, the innovations that can relieve the world's dependence on oil can be expected to emerge. The United States has the world's largest capital markets, the most populous and dynamic community of scientists, engineers, and inventors on the planet, and a long tradition of producing commercially viable innovations. A high American gasoline price will thus ultimately lead to the reduction of consumption not only in the United States but all over the world; and because, absent the relevant innovations, oil consumption will skyrocket in Asia, only reductions in oil consumption in all major countries will suffice to lower the global price and therefore the revenues accruing to the oil-exporters, thus ultimately easing the burden of American responsibilities in the Middle East and around the world.

None of this is either complicated or obscure, and the hazards of continuing high oil consumption and the benefits of reducing it are hardly a secret in the United States. The forty-third American president, George W. Bush, referred to his country's dependence on imported oil as an "addiction," thereby placing it in the unsavory company of alcoholism and the habitual ingestion of heroin. The geopolitical disease caused by oil dependence and the cure for this disease are both well known. Nor is it impossible for Western democracies to do what is necessary to cut back on oil consumption: the countries of Western Europe and Japan impose high taxes on gasoline. The United States, however, does not. Their European and Japanese counterparts pay two-and-one-half to three times as much for a gallon of gasoline as do Americans, and sometimes more. For Americans, not only in comparison with what the others pay but also in comparison with what their national interest and the interest of global security require, gasoline is ruinously cheap.

The collective failure of Americans to charge themselves as much for gasoline as is good for them (and for others) stems from several features of American society and its political culture: the long experience with inexpensive, and for decades American-produced, oil; the resistance to placing limits on consumption of any kind in what has historically been a land of plenty; the size and settlement patterns of the country, which embed long-distance driving deeply in the life of the nation; and the pronounced aversion, not found with anything like the same intensity in other democracies, to taxation of all kinds, which makes elected officials fearful of voting for even such an obviously necessary measure as a gasoline tax.

So widespread and deeply rooted is the American dislike of taxation that in 2009 the newly installed Obama administration, which, unlike its predecessor, was strongly committed to reducing the country's reliance on oil, chose as its method of doing so an administrative directive mandating higher gasoline mileage for new cars rather than a tax on gasoline. Increasing the CAFE (Corporate Average Fuel Economy) standard for cars sold in the United States is likely to curtail, to some extent, the American consumption of petroleum, but it is a far less effective and efficient way to accomplish this than a straightforward gasoline tax, something the administration did not even attempt to implement. Its secretary of energy, the Nobel Prize–winning physicist Steven Chu, who had outspokenly endorsed a gasoline tax while a private citizen, admitted shortly after taking office that such a tax was not politically feasible.

To be sure, the price of imported oil, and therefore of gasoline in the United States, is almost certain to rise, and perhaps rise sharply, during the second decade of the twenty-first century even without a gasoline tax. Market forces, in particular the rising demand in Asia as cars replace bicycles as the vehicle of choice and the slow decline in easily accessible supplies of oil, will surely accomplish that. This rise will produce some conservation and substitution in the United States. A market-driven increase in the oil price will serve American and global interests less well, however, than one engineered by the government, for two reasons.

First, market-driven price increases have historically been followed by declines. While it has risen
over the past three decades, the international oil price
has followed a seesaw path, rather than a smooth tra-
jectory, in an upward direction. When it has dipped,
some of the investments that have been made in the
technologies of conservation and substitution have
become unprofitable and were abandoned, while
other potential investments were simply not made. A
consistently high price would spur more investment.
Second, with a government-imposed tax or floor
price, much of the revenue from the sale of oil would
go to the government, and ultimately, in democracies,
to the people it governs. If the government decrees
that oil will cost $10 a barrel, for instance, and this
reduces consumption enough to depress the market
price to $5, the extra $5 goes to the public treasury.
By contrast, when the price is set by global supply and
demand, the revenue goes to the exporting countries:
if the price is $10 per barrel the Iranian, Venezuelan,
Russian, and Saudi regimes collect all $10. In the first
case, that is, American consumers pay themselves. In
the second they pay the Iranian mullahs and the pa-
trons of al Qaeda.

The national insistence on keeping gasoline cheap
in the United States is the single greatest failure of

twenty-first-century American foreign policy. It is not a failure of understanding or foresight. It is a failure of political will. Here, another comparison with the Cold War policy of containment is instructive. That policy was designed to avoid repeating the disastrous mistakes of the period between the two world wars, when the European democracies failed to address the threat that Hitler's Germany presented until it was too late to avoid a catastrophic war. Behind their interwar policy of appeasement lay their publics' reluctance to make modest sacrifices in order to stand up to Hitler in the short term, which would, in retrospect, have avoided the necessity of far larger sacrifices later, and their governments' reluctance to ask such sacrifices of them. The politics of oil in the United States operates according to the same dynamic, with the same disastrous consequences. The overall cost to Americans of their oil consumption, including the adverse geopolitical consequences, is higher than it would be if they were willing to tax gasoline more heavily, and that overall cost, absent such a tax, will only rise in the years ahead. In this sense cheap oil is the twenty-first-century equivalent of the European appeasement of the 1930s.

The advent of the Obama administration marked a watershed in the politics of American energy policy not only because the new president brought to office a greater determination to reduce the country's oil consumption than his predecessor had, but also because in 2009 the politics of oil policy merged with, and was submerged in, a larger issue: climate change. The accumulation in the earth's atmosphere of greenhouse gases, which prominently include the carbon gases emitted by the burning of fossil fuels, came to be widely regarded, at the end of the twentieth century and the beginning of the twenty-first, as causing a rise in the global temperature.

The warming of the planet is likely to have a variety of climatic, social, and political effects, none of them predictable with perfect accuracy but some of them all too likely to be disruptive and destructive of human life on Earth. All fossil fuels contribute to this greenhouse effect, so addressing climate change will require reductions in energy usage that go beyond oil to include natural gas and especially coal. In 2009, the first serious American effort to curtail the emission of greenhouse gases, including gasoline, made its way through the Congress, with the encouragement of the new administration.

For the purpose of reducing the consumption of oil in the United States the placement of gasoline within the political framework of climate change is a mixed blessing. On the one hand, this lends greater urgency to the cause. Using less gasoline becomes a way not only of enhancing American security policy but also of saving the entire planet, and the human species, from potential disaster: droughts, floods, storms, and other possible consequences of a rise in the earth's temperature. Accordingly, linking it to global warming broadens the coalition devoted to reducing gasoline consumption.

On the other hand, the sheer magnitude of the problem of climate change presents an obstacle to an effective political response to oil. The scope of the problem means that a comparably broad solution is required, one that will be more expensive for Americans and more disruptive to the American economy than simply curtailing the use of oil. The political coalition opposing dramatic steps to stop climate change is itself bound to be bigger and more powerful than the forces, formidable though they are, arrayed against raising the price of gasoline. The failure of the international climate change conference held in Copenhagen in December 2009 to set binding targets for the reduction of greenhouse gases demonstrated how difficult it will be to implement the measures, which would have to be global in scope, necessary to achieve sufficient reductions in the emission of these gases.

Moreover, because oil contributes only a part of the greenhouse gases that the United States emits, the legislative efforts to cut back on the emission of these gases will not be aimed exclusively at its use. One of the 2009 climate change bills in the House of Representatives would have raised the price of gasoline by only about 75 cents per gallon. To be sure, by American standards this would count as an appreciable increase, but it is one that would still leave Americans paying far less than the Western Europeans and the Japanese.

The American dependence on oil, with all the ill effects that follow from it, has the same fundamental cause as the impending economic constraints on American foreign policy and those who rely on it: the failure to pay the full costs of what is consumed. For energy, the American price of oil does not take account of what economists call externalities: costs associated with its use not captured by its selling price, in this case costs that include the impact both on the environment and on the protection of American interests in the Middle East and around the world. The real cost of a gallon of gasoline, for example—although not the price at the pump in the United States—properly includes the cost of the American military forces that ensure that it reaches the consumer. The fiscal policy of the United States (as well as the economic behavior of many households) has exhibited the same syndrome: the failure to pay the full cost of what the federal government does. In fiscal terms, the gap between what individuals and governments spend, on the one hand, and what individuals earn and governments collect in taxes, on the other, is bridged by borrowing.

Borrowed money ultimately has to be paid back, with interest, and so the resort to it, like the failure to reduce oil consumption and perhaps the failure to curb greenhouse gas emissions, simply postpones the day of reckoning and increases the price that has to be paid when that day arrives. September 15, 2008, is a red-letter day in the history of American foreign policy precisely because it marks the beginning of an extended day of fiscal reckoning, one that will impose new limits on the conduct of America's foreign relations.

If the fiscal problem and the oil problem are similar in structure, the solutions to them complement each other. The solution is straightforward in each case: the government needs to collect more revenue and individuals need to consume less oil. Taxing gasoline is a way to achieve both. Gasoline, moreover, has a distinct advantage over the American government's other two principal sources of revenue. The Social Security program draws its funding from a payroll tax. General government expenditures depend on the federal income tax. Raising these taxes, however, has negative economic consequences: curtailing job creation in the first case and, by some accounts, discouraging work in the second.

Furthermore, raising these two taxes would diminish the willingness of the American taxpayer, who will have to pay them, to continue to support the foreign policies on which global prosperity and stability have come to depend. The steep rises in the familiar forms of taxation that the events of September 15 and their aftermath portend, when they occur, will indirectly weaken the American global role and so make the world both a more dangerous and a far poorer place. A rising gasoline tax, however, would have the opposite effect. Because it would lower the American and the global consumption of oil and thus weaken the forces that threaten American and global interests in the Middle East and beyond, for Americans to pay more for gasoline would strengthen the role of the United States abroad and make the world a safer, wealthier place for almost everyone.

Conclusion

The most sweeping changes in international relations have come about as a direct result of the great wars of modern history. In the wake of the Napoleonic Wars of the late eighteenth and early nineteenth centuries, the two world wars of the first half of the twentieth century, and the Cold War, political systems and sovereign states with long histories were swept away and new ones were born, borders shifted, and some countries fell from the heights of international power while others replaced them at the top of the global hierarchy. The growing economic constraints on American foreign policy will not have such immediate, visibly dramatic effects, but like the great wars of the past, they too will change the world.

The impact of America's fiscal challenges will resemble, in some ways, the ebbing of British power. In the nineteenth century and for the first part of the twentieth, Great Britain deployed formidable military might and economic strength. With these assets, and especially through the possession of the largest empire and most capable navy on the planet, the British provided some of the global services that the United States furnished in the twenty-first. World War II accelerated the decline that had begun in the previous century, so that Great Britain was unable to contribute as it once had to international security and to the smooth functioning of the international economy.

The contraction of America's international role will not be as steep. The United States will remain, into the second decade of the twenty-first century and perhaps beyond, of all the countries in the world the one with the most capable military forces and largest economy. On the other hand, when Britain could no longer provide global governance the United States stepped in to replace it. No country now stands ready to replace the United States, so the loss to international peace and prosperity has the potential to be greater as America pulls back than when Britain did. For precisely this reason, the United

States will not give up all of its global responsibilities and abandon all of the missions it undertook in the wake of the Cold War, even as paying for them becomes increasingly difficult. It will, however, give up some of them.

The financial collapse of 2008 and the deep recession that followed have already eliminated one major economic role. With Americans spending less and saving more, the United States has ceased to be the world's consumer of last resort, on which other countries can rely to buy the products they made for export. The dollar remains the world's principal currency, but as much because of the lack of a viable substitute as because of global confidence in American economic dependability. The continuation of the special status of the American currency in world markets is far from assured.

The policy of using American military forces to protect people persecuted by their own governments, which the United States carried out in Somalia, Haiti, Bosnia, and Kosovo (and considered but rejected carrying out in Rwanda and Darfur), will not be repeated. Nor will the kind of strenuous effort to foster democracy that the American government undertook in Afghanistan and Iraq be repeated elsewhere, or even continued in those places indefinitely. Neither mission will earn the necessary political support from an inwardly preoccupied American public worried about increases in the costs and reductions in the benefits of entitlement programs.

The enterprise of state-building, to which the post–Cold War military interventions led, will disappear from the foreign policy agenda of the United States. At the beginning of the century's second decade this trend was already apparent. The dispatch from Yemen of a Nigerian terrorist to attempt to blow up an American airliner, and a destructive earthquake in Haiti, made those two countries prime candidates for American state-building efforts according to the criteria of the first two post–Cold War decades. Ten years earlier the United States might well have made such an effort in either or both places. In 2010, however, the political will and economic resources for the task were not available. State-building had become a luxury the United States could no longer afford. Accordingly, all the talk of reforming the agencies of the federal government—the State and Defense departments in particular—to equip them to create working institutions in poor, war-ravaged countries will remain just that: talk.

America's military interventions were intended to diminish oppression, relieve suffering, protect the innocent, and establish order and a measure of justice in the places where they occurred. At least to some extent, they succeeded. For those who might have hoped for comparable assistance from the United States in the future, but because of American economic constraints will not receive it, therefore, the world will be a more disorderly and dangerous place.

The impact of fiscally driven restraints on American foreign policy will go well beyond the end of deep involvement in the affairs of poor, distressed countries. As the country's fiscal condition deteriorates, political pressure in favor of a preference for butter over guns will grow, which will affect the defense budget. The political battles over how much to spend on defense will be intense ones because defense expenditures command both strong supporters—those who benefit from them will organize to lobby in favor of them—and strong arguments—most of the defense budget supports missions of greater importance to American and global security than humanitarian intervention and democracy promotion. Specifically, the personnel and weaponry that the defense budget goes to purchase make possible the American presence in three crucial regions, East Asia, Europe, and the Middle East, where three countries—China in the first, Russia in the second, and Iran in the third— have the potential to disrupt the peace on which the

United States and other countries of these regions, and indeed the whole world, depend.

Fortunately, the capacity for disruption is inversely related to the incentive for it: China could create economic, political, and even military havoc in East Asia but has powerful reasons not to do so. The Islamic Republic of Iran, by contrast, is determined to dominate the Persian Gulf region and the greater Middle East, but has only comparatively modest means to support its ongoing campaign to achieve this. In capabilities and intentions Russia falls between the two of them. Still, a challenge to regional peace and prosperity is possible in all three places, American power will remain the indispensable core of a successful response to any such challenge, and with the decline in resources available for projecting that power beyond the borders of the United States the American government will attempt, in all three regions, to enlist other counties to discourage and, if necessary, to resist dangerous initiatives.

In East Asia this trend is already under way. In response to China's rapid economic growth, Washington has sought to broaden its cooperation with the other Asian giant, India, in order to supplement its existing alliances with Australia, New Zealand, South Korea, and Japan and its ties with the countries of

Southeast Asia, all of which date from the Cold War (or in the case of communist Vietnam, from the first post-Cold War decade.) The United States and the countries of Asia disavow any intent to contain China, or to stifle its economic and political rise; and they would certainly prefer not to have to confront the People's Republic. Even if aggressive Chinese policies make confrontation seem necessary, China's large and growing economic importance will make its neighbors and trading partners reluctant to adopt explicitly anti-Chinese policies.

In Europe, the prospects for checking any Russian effort to overturn the political and economic status quo appear more promising. Not only is Russia weaker than China, and destined to grow weaker over time, but a European multilateral alliance that is more than six decades old already exists. NATO's ostensible twenty-first-century purpose is to promote democracy, not to contain Russia, but its eastern members joined precisely because they wanted the insurance they assumed the alliance would provide against unwanted attention from the Russians. It would be easy for NATO to resume its Cold War policy of containment, then directed against the Soviet Union, and apply it to post-communist Russia. It would not be easy, however, for such a policy to be effective. NATO, during the Cold War a robust multinational military organization, has now become a hollow shell. None of its members, including the United States, is prepared to deploy major military forces on the territories of its former Soviet-bloc members to check Russian military power, as NATO forces were deployed in large numbers in Germany to deter the Soviet Union during the Cold War.

The kind of diplomatic initiative most likely to strengthen the American position in Europe is one that would improve relations with Russia—which were on course for a productive partnership only to be derailed by the misguided decision to expand NATO eastward in the 1990s. For such an initiative to be successful, however, it was, at the beginning of the second decade of the twenty-first century, both too late and too soon. It was too late to avoid, or even mitigate, the damage to Russia's relations with the West that NATO expansion inflicted. It was too soon to reorient those relations in a fundamental way because that would require the replacement of the Putin regime in Moscow with one less resolutely hostile to the United States, a hostility that is deep enough to be part of the regime's basic political identity. That regime, with or without Vladimir Putin, will not last forever, but when and how it will change cannot be predicted. What can be safely predicted is that any such change will come from forces within Russia, and not by dint of pressures exerted by other countries.

The Middle East is the region that will most urgently require American power to counteract a threat because it is in that region that the threat is most acute. The Islamic Republic of Iran is deeply and openly committed to, and actively works for, overturning the existing political and economic arrangements there. It seeks to displace the United States as the region's most powerful country, to replace the governments of the Middle East with regimes that accept its primacy and, where possible, reproduce its own brand of Islamic fundamentalism, and to destroy the United Nations–created and internationally recognized sovereign state of Israel. The Iranian agenda is, in short, ambitious, specific, and pernicious.

An American military presence in some form will be necessary to deter Iran as long as the clerical regime holds power. Its aspirations for at least regional dominance are sufficiently virulent that the United States may find itself in open warfare with the mullahs and their armed forces. Of the three regions of the world of continuing strategic importance, moreover, the Middle East is the one with the least promising collection of potential allies. The Arab

countries that Iran has targeted are weak, with dicta-
torial governments that command little popular support, and are thus unlikely to be able to make
substantial political, let alone military, contributions
to their own defense. Muslim but non-Arab Turkey
has belonged to NATO for more than half a century,
but the assumption of power there by an Islamic political party has put in doubt its solidarity against Iran.
The United States will therefore increasingly cooperate with the only democratic and reliably pro-
American country in the Middle East, a country with
a legitimate government, a cohesive society, and formidable military forces: the state of Israel.

While the United States has only limited scope for
strengthening its position in the Middle East by con-
structing a broad coalition to oppose Iran, it is within
America's power to help stabilize the region in another way: by weakening Iran. The thus far unutilized
vehicle for achieving this aim, as well as for improving the American position in Europe, East Asia, and
other places, is a substantial reduction in American
oil consumption. Using less oil is the single measure
that would do the most to advance American interests
in the world. It is as central, in its way, to the twenty-
first-century pursuit of those interests as the policy
of containing the Soviet Union and international
communism was during the Cold War.

Lowering the world price of oil through a dramatic decrease in demand would reduce the resources at the disposal of the governments of both Iran and Russia, which depend on the sale of the oil within their borders for the funds that support the policies that the United States opposes. The United States can reduce its consumption of oil by raising the price of gasoline through a tax on it, which would motivate consumers to use less, mainly by driving fuel-efficient vehicles. Manufacturers would thus have an economic incentive—which is the only kind of incentive that counts in business—to develop and produce such vehicles. Once available, drivers all over the world would purchase them. Furthermore, a gasoline tax would send a great deal of money directly to the American treasury, which would help address the underlying cause of the ebbing of American foreign policy: the large and growing gap between the federal government's income and its entitlement-driven expenses.

A reduction in oil consumption through a sizable tax on gasoline in the United States would have yet a third, in this case political and symbolic, beneficial consequence for the American position in the world and for stability in East Asia, Europe, and the Middle East. It would demonstrate what has not been in evidence in the post–Cold War era: an American capacity for effective collective action to address a major problem. It would further demonstrate that the American people, through the establishment by their elected representatives of a major levy on an indispensable product, are capable of imposing short-term sacrifice on themselves in pursuit of a major international goal. It would demonstrate, finally, that the United States is capable of taking steps to deal with an issue that affects the entire world. It would offer, that is, a vivid example of American global leadership.

As such, it would enhance the image of the United States among friendly and unfriendly countries as a resolute and effective global leader. It would burnish the American reputation, which the international misadventures of the first two post–Cold War decades and the failure of the American financial system in 2008 have tarnished, for meeting challenges beyond its borders. This would reinforce the American position in the three key regions and diminish the likelihood that China, Russia, or Iran would mount a violent assault on it, because in international relations the image of and reputation for power form part of the substance of power itself, and the international order will continue to depend, for its stability, on American power.

Even if elected public officials in the United States should find a way to impose a steep tax on gasoline, however, the country's fiscal condition in the second decade of the twenty-first century and beyond will place unaccustomed constraints on American foreign policy. Here a final illustrative comparison can be made, to the circumstances of America's state and local governments in the wake of the financial crisis triggered by the events of September 15, 2008, and the deep recession that followed. With tax revenues sharply reduced by the economic downturn, they found themselves facing their own version of the federal government's gap between income and expenditures. The State of California faced a particularly large budget deficit. Unlike the federal government, however, states and municipalities cannot print the money they need to meet their obligations, and their capacity for borrowing to make up their shortfalls is far more limited than their federal counterpart's. They therefore had to reduce services. All over the United States, police forces were cut, library hours were curtailed, teachers from the elementary to the university levels were laid off, and public health facilities were closed.

Like American state and local governments to the citizens within their jurisdictions, the United States provides governmental services to the world. As the fiscal burden it must bear grows heavier, America, like California, will become less generous in furnishing these services. The world will thus get less, and less effective, governance. The precise consequences for global peace and prosperity cannot be foreseen, but they are not likely to be benign, and this will ensure that international politics will change in at least one noticeable way.

In the first decade of the twenty-first century, much of the world expressed—through rallies, speeches, petitions, and public opinion polls—its disapproval of a series of American foreign policies, above all the war in Iraq. They generally considered such policies to be the result of the United States' having too much power. In the century's second decade the economic conditions in which the United States will have to operate will lead to what are all too likely to be the far more disagreeable and globally damaging consequences of the United States' having too little power. One thing worse than an America that is too strong, the world will learn, is an America that is too weak.

Index

Atomic bomb, 103–104
Axis powers of World
     War II, 106–107,
     108–110
Aziz, King Abdul, 141

Baby-boom generation
  demographics and,
     22–26
  entitlement program
     costs and, 20–22
Balkan interventions, 89–90
Beckett, Samuel, 50
Beijing, China, 116–117,
     120, 122
Bilmes, Linda, 72
Bosnia, 42, 85–86, 89, 183
Bryan, William Jennings,
     27
Budget, American, 4, 49–52
  See also Economy,
     United States;
     Entitlement programs
Bush administration
  Afghanistan and, 43–44
  Arab-Israeli conflict and,
     153, 154–155, 156
  cardinal sin of, 91
  Iraq disaster of, 66
  Middle East hostility
     towards, 53

NATO expansion and,
     133
  See also Iraq, occupation
     of
Bush, George W.
  American foreign policy
     after Cold War and,
     41, 42
  oil and, 171

CAFE (Corporate Average
     Fuel Economy), 173
Chavez, Hugo, 161
China
  American debt and,
     15–16
  Cold War military
     initiatives of,
     119–120
  conclusions regarding,
     186–187
  cooperation and, 93–94
  currency of, 79–80
  economic contributions
     to armed forces of,
     115–116
  economic policies of,
     117–119
  Germany compared
     with, 113–114,
     121–122

© Anne Mandelbaum

Michael Mandelbaum is the Christian A. Herter Professor and Director of American Foreign Policy at The Johns Hopkins University School of Advanced International Studies (SAIS) in Washington D.C. He is a former faculty member at Harvard University, Columbia University, and The United States Naval Academy. He earned his Ph.D. in political science at Harvard University. He is the author or coauthor of eleven previous books, including *The Ideas That Conquered the World: Peace, Democracy, and Free Markets in the Twenty-first Century*; *The Case for Goliath: How America Acts as the World's Government in the Twenty-first Century*; and *Democracy's Good Name: The Rise and Risks of the World's Most Popular Form of Government*, all published by PublicAffairs.

PublicAffairs is a publishing house founded in 1997. It is a tribute to the standards, values, and flair of three persons who have served as mentors to countless reporters, writers, editors, and book people of all kinds, including me.

I. F. STONE, proprietor of *I. F. Stone's Weekly*, combined a commitment to the First Amendment with entrepreneurial zeal and reporting skill and became one of the great independent journalists in American history. At the age of eighty, Izzy published *The Trial of Socrates*, which was a national bestseller. He wrote the book after he taught himself ancient Greek.

BENJAMIN C. BRADLEE was for nearly thirty years the charismatic editorial leader of *The Washington Post*. It was Ben who gave the *Post* the range and courage to pursue such historic issues as Watergate. He supported his reporters with a tenacity that made them fearless and it is no accident that so many became authors of influential, best-selling books.

ROBERT L. BERNSTEIN, the chief executive of Random House for more than a quarter century, guided one of the nation's premier publishing houses. Bob was personally responsible for many books of political dissent and argument that challenged tyranny around the globe. He is also the founder and longtime chair of Human Rights Watch, one of the most respected human rights organizations in the world.

. . .

For fifty years, the banner of Public Affairs Press was carried by its owner Morris B. Schnapper, who published Gandhi, Nasser, Toynbee, Truman, and about 1,500 other authors. In 1983, Schnapper was described by *The Washington Post* as "a redoubtable gadfly." His legacy will endure in the books to come.

Peter Osnos, *Founder and Editor-at-Large*